Is Jesus God?

A Journal Bible Study Exploring God and Jesus with the Book of John

Sandy K. Cook

Published by Psalm 30 Publishing,
© 2020 Sandra K. Cook, All rights reserved.

Cover Photo Credit: https://www.pexels.com/@philippedonn "Lightning Strike on City," used under Free to use, public domain open license, with no attribution required.

ISBN: 978-1-948953-06-1

The contents of this book are protected by U.S. Copyright laws. No part of this book may be copied electronically, by photocopy, reproduced in digital format, or distributed by any means whatsoever without explicit written permission from Psalm 30 Publishing. Requests for permissions may be addressed to:

Psalm 30 Publishing,
P.O. Box 491328,
Lawrenceville, GA 30049

Unless otherwise noted, Bible verses printed in this book are taken from translations of the Bible that are in the Public Domain. Verses have been taken from an ASV-based, Public Domain translation, and have been modified to eliminate the use of the formal name of God. Within this book, God is addressed as God, The Lord, or Jesus throughout the book. As required by the Public Domain permissions of the secondary Public Domain source, the specific secondary Public Domain source will remain unidentified in this publication, because some verses have been modified and no longer directly reflect the content of the specific public domain source.

DEDICATION

This book is dedicated to my brothers and sisters in Christ who have gone before me in teaching younger generations about God and Jesus throughout the ages.

Specifically, I would like to honor Betty Barrow Varner of Atlanta, Georgia, who passed away at the age of 93. Betty was my first true Christian Mentor when I was a young adult struggling to understand God, Jesus, the Holy Spirit, the trilogy, sanctification, edification, salvation, and a whole host of other concepts that are foreign to any person not raised in the church.

Betty was my next door neighbor for a season when I first moved to the Metro Atlanta area. She was a joyful, loving Christian woman who set an example of being a Titus 2:3-5 daughter of God. I aim to humbly come along the same road Betty traveled, sharing the love and joy of Jesus with younger women who are seeking truth and light to live by.

Table of Contents

A LOOK BEFORE YOU LEAP 1
CHAPTER 1 9
CHAPTER 2 17
CHAPTER 3 23
CHAPTER 4 31
CHAPTER 5 39
CHAPTER 6 47
CHAPTER 7 57
CHAPTER 8 65
CHAPTER 9 75
CHAPTER 10 83
CHAPTER 11 91
CHAPTER 12 99
CHAPTER 13 107
CHAPTER 14 115
CHAPTER 15 123
CHAPTER 16 129
CHAPTER 17 135
CHAPTER 18 141
CHAPTER 19 149
CHAPTER 20 157
CHAPTER 21 163
BONUS CHAPTERS: HEBREWS 1 & 2 171
WHAT'S NEXT? 179
ABOUT THE AUTHOR 183
OTHER BOOKS BY SANDY K. COOK 185

A LOOK BEFORE YOU LEAP

How Can We Know If Jesus Really Is GOD?

You may wonder why some people think Jesus is God, and whether we can know if Jesus is God. Jesus came to the world as a man in the flesh to show us the truth and the way to eternal life through Himself. In doing so, Jesus indicates He and God are one.

This Journal Bible Study will explore the Gospel Book of John, written by Jesus's disciple, John. There is deep theology in the Book of John, which many scholars study.

Explanations about who Jesus and God are, and the relationship between the two, are a primary focus in the Gospel of John. We'll look at the themes in the book of John and what Jesus says about Himself, the world, and eternal life.

While some feel they know Jesus IS God, others draw different conclusions from the Bible. This Journal Bible study doesn't come to a particular conclusion. Instead, this study points out what the scriptures say. The study will pose points and questions for you to consider, and lets you draw your own conclusions.

In other words, this study is a survey of what we KNOW Jesus said about Himself and His relationship with God. It's not a deep, brainy theological analysis of every statement and word. I don't think we need that type of depth to understand who Jesus is. Yet, we do need to grasp what Jesus tells us is "most certain" and what He says we must believe.

My hope is that you will gain appreciation for the divinity of Jesus, whether you believe He is actually God or not. Let's talk more about the study itself.

Why the Gospel of John?

The Gospel of John is like a theology book in a lot of ways. Within John's Gospel, Jesus tells us what to believe, who He is, and why God sent Jesus. The book provides specifics about what Jesus tells us to believe woven throughout it.

Key themes within the Gospel of John are:

1. **Belief** (mentioned 119 times),
2. The **World** (mentioned 78 times),
3. What is "certain" (with 25 "**most certain**" facts from Jesus),
4. Jesus's **I AM** declarations about who He is (7 times), and
5. And, who John says Jesus is.

Also within the Gospel is the concept of the Trinity or the godhead. It is a difficult concept to grasp. I liken it to our roles as someone's son or daughter, but also as a parent to our child(ren), and as someone's spouse. We are one person, but we have different relational roles. Our roles vary, depending on whether we are currently serving as a son or daughter, as a parent, or as a spouse. We are three different people, but one person.

God is one, but He is also the Father, the Son, and the Holy Spirit. Thus it's conceivable that God the Father can be the same as Jesus the Son. Yet, it's a difficult concept to grasp when it comes to talking about the Holy Trinity. God is the spiritual Father, the Holy Spirit is spirit, and Jesus is a physical and spiritual man.

If you know God can create physical things, then it's possible for Him to present Himself as a physical man. In this way, we know God can be the physical man Jesus, yet He can still be our Holy God. Psalm 100:3 says, "Know that the Lord Himself is God."

Let me give you an important preliminary bit of knowledge for this study. In the ancient days, before Jesus was born, God and Moses had the following exchange (Exodus 3:13-15):

"Moses said to God, 'Behold, when I come to the children of Israel, and tell them, 'The God of your fathers has sent me to you,' and they ask me, 'What is his name?' what should I tell them?'

"God said to Moses, 'I AM WHO I AM,' and he said, 'You shall tell the children of Israel this: 'I AM has sent me to you.'' God said moreover to Moses, 'You shall tell the children of Israel this, 'The Lord, the God of your fathers, the God of Abraham, the God of Isaac, and the God of Jacob, has sent me to you.' This is my name forever, and this is my memorial to all generations."

This fact about God calling Himself "I AM" is a baseline bit of theology before we dive into the Book of John. God calling Himself "I AM" may help you see the basis for some of what the Gospel of John says about Jesus being God.

What Kind of Bible Study is This?

This is an open-ended, reflective, and life-application Journal Bible Study. It's a combination book, journal, and workbook.

The study is open-ended and reflective, because it lets God's Holy Spirit teach you what He wants YOU to know. Many of the questions will help you explore how God's Word applies to your individual life.

In this study, you won't find long explanations about the passage's meanings. You won't find strong direction telling you what to think about Jesus, God, or the verses. Instead, I you encourage to pray and ask God for insight into His Word, as it applies to you in your life.

If you are in a Bible study group, discussing each person's insights can be eye-opening. That's because everyone gains different insights from a study like this.

Feel free to use online searches and Bible Commentaries to answer your questions. You can also gain understanding by rereading the texts as needed. If you're in a Bible study group, discuss questions you have with group members.

God made the Bible to understandable to common people. Thus, everyone will gain a measure of personal insight from this study. What you get out of each chapter will be between you and God. Your takeaways will depend on your life circumstances. It will also depend on whether you seek to understand God's Word.

This is a God-directed Bible study. In other words, as you read, pray and ask God for insight. Ask Him to show you the things He wants you to see. God will bring to your mind ideas and truths that are meaningful to you.

One of the main features of this Bible study is that it includes all the chapters of the Gospel of John. All you need is this book, a pen or pencil, and time to read and relate to God's Word.

Including the entire Book of John in this workbook serves two purposes. It makes studying more convenient. You won't have to go back-and-forth between a workbook, journal, and your Bible. You can read the text and answer the questions in this workbook journal.

The second purpose for including the full text is for simplicity in studying. It can be difficult and time consuming to locate passages in a Bible. That's especially true if you're new to Bible study or unfamiliar with the Bible. Having to look up scriptures can affect your ability to grasp the deeper meaning in the verses.

By including the Bible text in this Journal, you can read without stopping. Thus, the design of this Journal Bible Study is made to be pain free—easy to use and easy to understand.

On a side note: even though this study includes the full Gospel of John, it's good for you to have an actual Bible to read too. This Journal Bible Study series makes studying individual books of the Bible easier. It does this by covering one book at a time. But, the studies aren't God's complete works. A deep understanding of God can't be found in isolation from the rest of the Bible. All the Bible, taken as a whole, is critical for understanding God.

If you don't have your own Bible, or aren't sure how to choose a translation that is easy for you to read, visit: http://christianonlinebiblestudy.com/how-to-choose-a-bible/.

The information on that webpage shows you how to select a version that is easy for you to use. There are samples of different translations, so you can pick the one you like best. You can find a translation that is easy for you to read.

How To Use This Journal Bible Study

In this Journal Bible Study, each chapter covers one chapter in the Gospel of the Book of John. There are no verse numbers, since John wrote his story as a book without numbered verses. Removing verse numbers lets your reading flow. You can read John's story as it was written.

Next to each column of story text, there is a wide margin for your note taking or journaling. The margin lets you write anything that comes to mind as you read. You can use the journal area to make notes about:

➢ Questions you have,
➢ Your emotions and reactions,
➢ Your thoughts about Jesus' teachings and actions,
➢ Your reaction to Jesus' commands,
➢ How you feel the text relates to your life or your personal character,
➢ Or any thought which you have while you're reading.

If you like to draw or color, the open space allows freedom to interact with the Bible text in any way you find helpful. You can highlight, underline, draw arrows, mark things up, and write whatever comes to mind. Reading actively will help you remember what you're reading.

The best way to use this study is to settle in where you'll be comfortable and read a chapter. Before you begin reading, take a few minutes to pray. Praying is talking to God, as if He were a friend sitting next to you. Since God is Spirit, He is with us at all times wherever we go. He will hear whatever you say or ask. You may want to pray something like this:

" Dear Lord, please open my mind and heart to understand that which you want me to learn through this study today. Give me the knowledge and understanding I need. Please speak to my heart and touch me where I need it. Help me see Jesus for who He is, and reveal Yourself to me. I ask these things in the name of Jesus, Amen."

At the end of each chapter, you will find a "**WHAT DO YOU THINK?**" section. This is an opportunity to explore how the chapter's content applies to you.

Take the scriptures into your heart. Consider what the Bible verses mean to you. Ask God what He wants YOU to know, then answer each of the questions as you feel led.

Make this study personal. Make it about you and your relationship with God. Take time to think about what you're reading and how you want to respond.

If you have no immediate reaction or thought, pray over the question. Ask God for His insight. Ask Him to bring to your mind ideas about how the chapter and prophecies apply to you.

Quiet your spirit for a moment, and wait for meaningful insight to come into your mind. Take note of any thoughts the Holy Spirit brings to you. Pause and reflect on the questions, so meaningful things come to your mind.

On that note, "What's next?" for your first chapter of this Journal Bible Study?

The Gospel of John begins by telling us who is Jesus, but John calls Jesus "The Word." In the first paragraph, John tells us, "The Word was God." From the symbolism of "The Word," we know Jesus is the Word, and The Word was God. From the first paragraph onward, our understanding of Jesus, the Word, and God grows.

Major Themes in This Book

There are four major themes in the Gospel of John which focus on who is Jesus and why did he come to us. You will find many direct teachings of Jesus where He tells us what is "most certain." He tells us what we must believe, about who He is, and His eternal impact on the world.

In the first theme, Jesus makes seven explicit **I AM** declarations about who He is. There are several other declarations also. Jesus tells us plainly who He is and why He came, if we choose to believe He's telling the truth.

For each of the explicit declarations Jesus makes about himself, I have bolded the words "**I AM**." The Bold text acts as a marker to capture your attention, so you won't miss the declaration Jesus is making.

For the second theme, Jesus declares things that are "most certain." Jesus says, "**most certainly**" 27 times. These are definitive facts about Jesus's purpose and our salvation. Jesus makes other critical points He wants us to understand too. Jesus's "**most certainly**" statements are in bold text as an attention marker.

There are the 119 **Believe** statements made throughout the book. It is the third and most frequently occurring theme. Jesus tells us clearly what we are to believe.

Lastly, the fourth theme focuses on what Jesus has to say about the world. The word "**world**" occurs 90 times in the Gospel of John. It is also printed in bold text to draw your attention to the point Jesus is making about the world.

These four major themes are the foundation for the Gospel of John's focus on Jesus's ministry on earth. They are important for us to know and understand Jesus's mission.

As a brief aside, before diving into the study, let's see who was John, besides the author of the Book of John.

Who Was John?

John was a Jewish man selected by Jesus as an apostle. John and his brother James were two fishermen who followed Jesus. They lived and traveled with Jesus throughout Jesus's life. John became a beloved "disciple whom Jesus loved" (John 13:23).

The Gospel of John's Authority

An Apostle who was selected by Jesus and traveled with Jesus wrote the Gospel of John. Thus, the Book of John contains a unique perspective. It has definitive authority about Jesus, because John is an Apostle Jesus knew and loved. John's theological insight and teachings are unique among the four Gospels.

The four Gospel books (Matthew, Mark, Luke, and John) in the New Testament are early, authentic books. Other first century writers reference these Gospel books. These early references show all the Gospels were written when people who actually knew Jesus were alive.

We have more supporting evidence for the authenticity of the Gospels than we do for other early writings. Caesar, Plato, Aristotle, and other early writers don't have as much supporting evidence. Thus, the Gospels are reliable documents about Jesus. (Visit https://carm.org/manuscript-evidence to learn more about dating of the Gospel manuscripts.)

Your belief about whether Jesus is God (or not) depends on whether you believe what's written. Will you believe the Gospel authors like you believe Caesar, Plato, and Aristotle?

Your outcome depends on whether you pray for insight and understanding from God as you read. It will also depend upon the personal insights God gives you. The impact of this study also depends on how deep is your desire for a connection with God. Your openness toward learning whatever God wants you to learn is a key factor too.

In Matthew 7:7 Jesus tells us, "Ask, and it will be given you. Seek, and you will find. Knock, and it will be opened for you." So ASK God to help you see the truth in His Word, and seek understanding of God and Jesus through this study.

My hope is that you will receive the news of Jesus as a REAL man with joy and clarity through this Journal Bible Study. I hope you're inspired by the Gospel message and find this is a worthwhile journey through the Book of John.

As you read, remember, praying to God is like talking to a good friend sitting next to you. Whether you speak aloud, or whether you express yourself to God with words in your mind, He hears you. This means, at any point in your reading, you can stop and pray. Doing so will help you gain deeper understanding.

Are you ready to learn *Is Jesus God*?

Let's dive into the book and prophecies to discover what God wants you to know. Remember "*the Word*" in the first paragraph is Jesus, according to scholars who study the Bible..

CHAPTER 1

In the beginning was the Word, and the Word was with God, and the Word was God. The same was in the beginning with God. All things were made through him.

Without him, nothing was made that has been made. In him was life, and the life was the light of men. The light shines in the darkness, and the darkness hasn't overcome it. There came a man, sent from God, whose name was John. The same came as a witness, that he might testify about the light, that all might **believe** through him. He was not the light, but was sent that he might testify about the light. The true light that enlightens everyone was coming into the **world**.

He was in the **world**, and the **world** was made through him, and the **world** didn't recognize him. He came to his own, and those who were his own didn't receive him. But as many as received him, to them he gave the right to become God's children, to those who **believe** in his name: who were born not of blood, nor of the will of the flesh, nor of the will of man, but of God.

The Word became flesh, and lived among us. We saw his glory, such glory as of the one and only Son of the Father, full of grace and truth. John testified about him. He cried out, saying, "This was he of whom I said, 'He who comes after me has surpassed me, for he was before me.'" From his fullness we all received grace upon grace. For the law was given through Moses. Grace and truth were realized through Jesus Christ. No one has seen God at any time. The one and only Son, who is in the bosom of the Father, has declared him.

This is John's testimony, when the Jews sent priests and Levites from Jerusalem to ask him, "Who are you?"

He declared, and didn't deny, but he declared, "I am not the Christ."

They asked him, "What then? Are you Elijah?"

He said, "I am not." "Are you the prophet?" He answered, "No."

They said therefore to him, "Who are you? Give us an answer to take back to those who sent us. What do you say about yourself?"

He said, "I am the voice of one crying in the wilderness, 'Make straight the way of the Lord,' as Isaiah the prophet said."

The ones who had been sent were from the Pharisees. They asked him, "Why then do you baptize, if you are not the Christ, nor Elijah, nor the prophet?"

John answered them, "I baptize in water, but among you stands one whom you don't know. He is the one who comes after me, who is preferred before me, whose sandal strap I'm not worthy to loosen." These things were done in Bethany beyond the Jordan, where John was baptizing.

The next day, he saw Jesus coming to him, and said, "Behold, the Lamb of God, who takes away the sin of the **world**! This is he of whom I said, 'After me comes a man who is preferred before me, for he was before me.' I didn't know him, but for this reason I came baptizing in water: that he would be revealed to Israel."

John testified, saying, "I have seen the Spirit descending like a dove out of heaven, and it remained on him. I didn't recognize him, but he who sent me to baptize in water said to me, 'On whomever you will see the Spirit descending and remaining on him is he who baptizes in the Holy Spirit.' I have seen, and have testified that this is the Son of God."

Again, the next day, John was standing with two of his disciples, and he looked at Jesus as he walked, and said, "Behold, the Lamb of God!" The two disciples heard him speak, and they followed Jesus. Jesus turned and saw them following, and said to them, *"What are you looking for?"*

They said to him, "Rabbi" (which is to say, being interpreted, Teacher), "where are you staying?"

He said to them, *"Come, and see."*

They came and saw where he was staying, and they stayed with him that day. It was about the tenth hour. One of the two who heard John and followed him was Andrew, Simon Peter's brother. He first found his own brother, Simon, and said to him, "We have found the Messiah!" (which is, being interpreted, Christ).

He brought him to Jesus. Jesus looked at him, and said, *"You are Simon the son of Jonah. You shall be called Cephas"* (which is by interpretation, Peter).

On the next day, he was determined to go out into Galilee, and he found Philip. Jesus said to him, *"Follow me."*

Now Philip was from Bethsaida, of the city of Andrew and Peter. Philip found Nathanael, and said to him, "We have found him, of whom Moses in the law, and the prophets, wrote: Jesus of Nazareth, the son of Joseph."

Nathanael said to him, "Can any good thing come out of Nazareth?"

Philip said to him, "Come and see."

Jesus saw Nathanael coming to him, and said about him, *"Behold, an Israelite indeed, in whom is no deceit!"*

Nathanael said to him, "How do you know me?"

Jesus answered him, *"Before Philip called you, when you were under the fig tree, I saw you."*

Nathanael answered him, "Rabbi, you are the Son of God! You are King of Israel!"

Jesus answered him, *"Because I told you, 'I saw you underneath the fig tree,'* *do you **believe**? You will see greater things than these!"* He said to him, *"**Most certainly**, I tell you all, hereafter you will see heaven opened, and the angels of God ascending and descending on the Son of Man."*

GOD AND JESUS REVELATIONS

In chapter one, we see, "the Word was with God and the Word was God. And the same was in the beginning with God, and all things were made through Him." So if Jesus is the Word, and He makes all things, then it is a logically sound argument that Jesus is God and God is Jesus.

It also says that, "In Him was life, and the life was the light of men." Genesis 2:7 says, "God formed man from the dust of the ground, and breathed into his nostrils the breath of life; and man became a living soul." So God and Jesus both give life to people.

These scriptures also say, "He was in the world, and the world was made through Him." Genesis 1 says, "In the beginning, God created the heavens and the earth." If we apply rules of logic and reasoning, we understand: If Jesus made the earth and God made the earth, Jesus (the Word) and God must the same person.

In verse 12, Jesus gave people the right to become children of God. So Jesus has the ability to grant us adoption into God's family. Thus, Jesus has authority to say who is in God's family and who is not.

In the first full paragraph on page ten, we also read the Word became flesh and made His dwelling among us. He was the one and only who came from the Father; the scripture refers to Jesus as, "God, the one and only." The verses at the beginning of the chapter are explicit about Jesus being God, and the One and Only.

Yet, these scriptures also talk about Jesus being at the Father's side and coming from the Father. Thus, it is clear that God the Father and Jesus God are two separate beings. They are one and the same, but separate and different. It's confusing!

IS JESUS GOD?

➢ In this chapter, what does John the Baptist say about God, the Father?

➢ In this chapter, what declarations does John the Baptist make about Jesus?

WHAT DO YOU THINK?

➢ At the beginning of this chapter, to your best ability, rewrite the first paragraph in plain words. Write as if you are explaining the paragraph to a 10 year-old child.

➢ What do you think light and darkness represent in this chapter's second paragraph?

➢ Why do you think people in the world didn't (don't) recognize who Jesus is?

➢ According to this chapter, what is required for a person to become a child of God?

➢ How would you describe the relationship of Jesus to God, as described in this chapter?

➤ What metaphors and phrases are used to describe Jesus in this chapter?

➤ What keeps people from recognizing Jesus as a light to the world in today's Society?

➤ What does Jesus want you to believe in this chapter?

➤ What does Jesus tell us about the world in this chapter?

CHAPTER 2

The third day, there was a wedding in Cana of Galilee.

Jesus' mother was there. Jesus also was invited, with his disciples, to the wedding. When the wine ran out, Jesus' mother said to him, "They have no wine."

Jesus said to her, *"Woman, what does that have to do with you and me? My hour has not yet come."*

His mother said to the servants, "Whatever he says to you, do it." Now there were six water pots of stone set there after the Jews' way of purifying, containing two or three metretes apiece.

Jesus said to them, *"Fill the water pots with water."* So they filled them up to the brim. He said to them, *"Now draw some out, and take it to the ruler of the feast."*

So they took it. When the ruler of the feast tasted the water now become wine, and didn't know where it came from (but the servants who had drawn the water knew), the ruler of the feast called the bridegroom and said to him, "Everyone serves the good wine first, and when the guests have drunk freely, then that which is worse. You have kept the good wine until now!" This beginning of his signs Jesus did in Cana of Galilee, and revealed his glory; and his disciples **believed** in him.

After this, he went down to Capernaum, he, and his mother, his brothers, and his disciples; and they stayed there a few days. The Passover of the Jews was at hand, and Jesus went up to Jerusalem. He found in the temple those who sold oxen, sheep, and doves, and the changers of money sitting. He made a whip of cords, and threw all out of the temple, both the sheep and the oxen; and he poured out the changers' money and overthrew their tables. To those who sold the doves, he said, *"Take these things out of here! Don't make my Father's house a marketplace!"* His disciples remembered that it was written, "Zeal for your house will eat me up."

The Jews therefore answered him, "What sign do you show us, seeing that you do these things?"

Jesus answered them, *"Destroy this temple, and in three days I will raise it up."*

The Jews therefore said, "It took forty-six years to build this temple! Will you raise it up in three days?" But he spoke of the temple of his body. When therefore he was raised from the dead, his disciples remembered that he said this, and they **believed** the Scripture, and the word which Jesus had said.

Now when he was in Jerusalem at the Passover, during the feast, many **believed** in his name, observing his signs which he did. But Jesus didn't entrust himself to them, because he knew everyone, and because he didn't need for anyone to testify concerning man; for he himself knew what was in man.

GOD AND JESUS REVELATIONS

In chapter two, Jesus declares, "Destroy this temple in three days and I will rebuild it." John mentions Jesus's resurrection afterwards, since John wrote his Gospel after Jesus's resurrection.

Through Jesus's declaration about raising Himself from the dead, we see evidence of Jesus's power over life and death. Since Jesus gives life, we know—at a minimum—Jesus has power to give life like God does.

IS JESUS GOD?

➢ Why do you think Jesus is so angry about people buying and selling in God's house?

➢ Do you think people have reverence for the house of God today? Why or why not?

WHAT DO YOU THINK?

➢ In this chapter, how does Mary demonstrate total faith in Jesus' abilities? How do people demonstrate faith in Jesus today?

_____
_____
_____
_____
_____

➢ Do Jesus's miracles in this chapter convince you of His divinity? Why or why not?

_____
_____
_____
_____
_____

➢ What abilities and powers does Jesus demonstrate through miracles and resurrection?

_____
_____
_____
_____
_____

➢ When Jesus says, "Destroy this Temple, and in three days I will raise it," He is talking about raising His body. Thus, Jesus can raise Himself from the dead. Compare Jesus' capabilities and characteristics to God's as they relate to life, death, and creation.

_____
_____
_____
_____
_____

➤ Who do people think Jesus is in this chapter?

➤ People believe in Jesus when they observe His signs (miracles). What signs or miracles do you expect to see from someone claiming to be God's Son or the Messiah?

➤ What do you think Jesus knew about the hearts of men, which kept Him from entrusting Himself to anyone?

CHAPTER 3

Now there was a man of the Pharisees named Nicodemus, a ruler of the Jews. The same came to him by night, and said to him, "Rabbi, we know that you are a teacher come from God, for no one can do these signs that you do, unless God is with him."

Jesus answered him, *"**Most certainly**, I tell you, unless one is born anew, he can't see God's Kingdom."*

Nicodemus said to him, "How can a man be born when he is old? Can he enter a second time into his mother's womb, and be born?"

Jesus answered, *"**Most certainly** I tell you, unless one is born of water and spirit, he can't enter into God's Kingdom. That which is born of the* *flesh is flesh. That which is born of the Spirit is spirit. Don't marvel that I said to you, 'You must be born anew.' The wind blows where it wants to, and you hear its sound, but don't know where it comes from and where it is going. So is everyone who is born of the Spirit."*

Nicodemus answered him, "How can these things be?"

Jesus answered him, *"Are you the teacher of Israel, and don't understand these things?* **Most certainly** *I tell you, we speak that which we know, and testify of that which we have seen, and you don't receive our witness.*

If I told you earthly things and you don't **believe***, how will you* **believe** *if I tell you heavenly things? No one has ascended into heaven but he who descended out of heaven, the Son of Man, who is in heaven. As Moses lifted up the serpent in the wilderness, even so must the Son of Man be lifted up, that whoever* **believes** *in him should not perish, but have eternal life. For God so loved the* **world***, that he gave his one and only Son, that whoever* **believes** *in him should not perish, but have eternal life. For God didn't send his Son into the* **world** *to judge the* **world***, but that the* **world** *should be saved through him. He who* **believes** *in him is not judged.*

He who doesn't **believe** *has been judged already, because he has not* **believed** *in the name of the one and only Son of God. This is the judgment, that the light has come into the* **world***, and men loved the darkness rather than the light; for their works were evil.*

For everyone who does evil hates the light, and doesn't come to the light, lest his works would be exposed. But he who does the truth comes to the light, that his works may be revealed, that they have been done in God."

After these things, Jesus came with his disciples into the land of Judea. He stayed there with them and baptized. John also was baptizing in Enon near Salim, because there was much water there. They came, and were baptized; for John was not yet thrown into prison. Therefore a dispute arose on the part of John's disciples with some Jews about purification. They came to John and said to him, "Rabbi, he who was with you beyond the Jordan, to whom you have testified, behold, he baptizes, and everyone is coming to him."

John answered, "A man can receive nothing unless it has been given him from heaven. You yourselves testify that I said, 'I am not the Christ,' but, 'I have been sent before him.' He who has the bride is the bridegroom; but the friend of the bridegroom, who stands and hears him, rejoices greatly because of the bridegroom's voice. This, my joy, therefore is made full. He must increase, but I must decrease. He who comes from above is above all. He who is from the earth belongs to the earth and speaks of the earth. He who comes from heaven is above all. What he has seen and heard, of that he testifies; and no one receives his witness. He who has received his witness has set his seal to this, that God is true. For he whom God has sent speaks the words of

God; for God gives the Spirit without measure. The Father loves the Son, and has given all things into his hand. One who believes in the Son has eternal life, but one who disobeys the Son won't see life, but the wrath of God remains on him."

GOD AND JESUS REVELATIONS

In chapter three, Jesus tells us what we must be born again of the spirit. Thus, a person has to be born twice in life—first being born of water (physical body), then born in the spirit. As people, we are physically born first, then we experience a spiritual birth or awakening.

Jesus, was spiritual first, but came to Earth to be born as a physical person, and mediator between God and man. Jesus and all people are both biological and spiritual. Thus, there's a unique relationship between Jesus and Born Again Christians.

The Bible says people who aren't born spiritually have an inability to grasp spiritual matters. This single factor keeps people from understanding Jesus Christ unless they are born again.

IS JESUS GOD?

➢ In this chapter, what declarations does Jesus make about Himself?

➢ What three things does Jesus say are "most certain" in this chapter?

WHAT DO YOU THINK?

➢ What does Jesus tell us to believe in this chapter?

_____
_____
_____
_____
_____
_____
_____

➢ In this chapter, Jesus declares His Good News to Nicodemus about being born again. In your own words, explain the Good News as if you're explaining it to someone else.

_____
_____
_____
_____
_____
_____
_____

➢ How would you explain what you believe about Jesus, based on what Jesus taught in this chapter?

_____
_____
_____
_____
_____
_____
_____

➤ Jesus mentions the world five times in this chapter. What does Jesus want us to know and understand about this world?

➤ Jesus explains the concept of the spirit being separate from the flesh. Can our ability to think be explained by cellular science alone? As best you can, explain how you think individual cells in the brain create our thoughts and personality.

➤ What are your thoughts about how one is Born Again of the spirit?

➢ What do you think happens within a person's Spirit when they are born again?

___

➢ Jesus talks about being the Son of God, ascending and descending from heaven, being sent by God and doing things "in God." Describe the roles of God and Jesus based on what we've read so far in this study?

___

➢ According To Jesus, for what purposes did God send Jesus to Earth?

___

CHAPTER 4

Therefore when the Lord knew that the Pharisees had heard that Jesus was making and baptizing more disciples than John (although Jesus himself didn't baptize, but his disciples), he left Judea and departed into Galilee. He needed to pass through Samaria. So he came to a city of Samaria, called Sychar, near the parcel of ground that Jacob gave to his son, Joseph. Jacob's well was there. Jesus therefore, being tired from his journey, sat down by the well. It was about the sixth hour. A woman of Samaria came to draw water. Jesus said to her, *"Give me a drink."* For his disciples had gone away into the city to buy food.

The Samaritan woman therefore said to him, "How is it that you, being a Jew, ask for a drink from me, a Samaritan woman?"

(For Jews have no dealings with Samaritans.)

Jesus answered her, *"If you knew the gift of God, and who it is who says to you, 'Give me a drink,' you would have asked him, and he would have given you living water."*

The woman said to him, "Sir, you have nothing to draw with, and the well is deep. So where do you get that living water? Are you greater than our father, Jacob, who gave us the well and drank from it himself, as did his children and his livestock?"

Jesus answered her, *"Everyone who drinks of this water will thirst again, but whoever drinks of the water that I will give him will never thirst again; but the water that I will give him will become in him a well of water springing up to eternal life."*

The woman said to him, "Sir, give me this water, so that I don't get thirsty, neither come all the way here to draw."

Jesus said to her, *"Go, call your husband, and come here."*

The woman answered, "I have no husband."

Jesus said to her, *"You said well, 'I have no husband,' for you have had five husbands; and he whom you now have is not your husband. This you have said truly."*

The woman said to him, "Sir, I perceive that you are a prophet. Our fathers worshiped in this mountain, and you Jews say that in Jerusalem is the place where people ought to worship."

Jesus said to her, *"Woman, **believe** me, the hour comes, when neither in this mountain, nor in Jerusalem, will you worship the Father. You worship that which you don't know. We worship that which we know; for salvation is from the Jews. But the hour comes, and now is, when the true worshipers will worship the Father in spirit and truth, for the Father seeks such to be his worshipers. God is spirit, and those who worship him must worship in spirit and truth."*

The woman said to him, "I know that Messiah comes, he who is called Christ. When he has come, he will declare to us all things."

Jesus said to her, *"I am he, the one who speaks to you."* At this, his disciples came. They marveled that he was speaking with a woman; yet no one said, "What are you looking for?" or, "Why do you speak with her?" So the woman left her water pot, went away into the city, and said to the people, "Come, see a man who told me everything that I did. Can this be the Christ?"

They went out of the city, and were coming to him. In the meanwhile, the disciples urged him, saying, "Rabbi, eat."

But he said to them, *"I have food to eat that you don't know about."*

The disciples therefore said to one another, "Has anyone brought him something to eat?"

Jesus said to them, *"My food is to do the will of him who sent me and to accomplish his work. Don't you say, 'There are yet four months until the harvest?' Behold, I tell you, lift up your eyes and look at the fields, that they are white for harvest already. He who reaps receives wages and gathers fruit to eternal life; that both he who sows and he who reaps may rejoice together. For in this the saying is true, 'One sows, and another reaps.' I sent you to reap that for which you haven't labored. Others have labored, and you have entered into their labor."*

From that city many of the Samaritans **believed** in him because of the word of the woman, who testified, "He told me everything that I did." So when the Samaritans came to him, they begged him to stay with them. He stayed there two days. Many more **believed** because of his word. They said to the woman, "Now we **believe**, not because of your speaking; for we have heard for ourselves, and know that this is indeed the Christ, the Savior of the **world**."

After the two days he went out from there and went into Galilee. For Jesus himself testified that a prophet has no honor in his own country. So when he came into Galilee, the Galileans received him, having seen all the things that he did in Jerusalem at the feast, for they also went to the feast. Jesus came therefore again to Cana of Galilee, where he made the water into wine. There was a certain nobleman whose son was sick at Capernaum. When he heard that Jesus had come out of Judea into Galilee, he went to him, and begged him that he would come down and heal his son, for he was at the point of death. Jesus therefore said to him, *"Unless you see signs and wonders, you will in no way believe."*

The nobleman said to him, "Sir, come down before my child dies." Jesus said to him, *"Go your way. Your son lives."* The man **believed** the word that Jesus spoke to him, and he went his way. As he was now going down, his servants met him and reported, saying "Your child lives!" So he inquired of them the hour when he began to get better. They said therefore to him, "Yesterday at the seventh hour, the fever left him." So the father knew that it was at that hour in which Jesus said to him, *"Your son lives."* He **believed**, as did his whole house.

This is again the second sign that Jesus did, having come out of Judea into Galilee.

GOD AND JESUS REVELATIONS

In this chapter, Jesus treats the Samaritan woman with dignity and respect. Her background would cause many other people to shun her. Consider how Jesus's knowledge about the woman and His concern for her reflect the character of God.

The woman at the well states the Messiah is coming, and Jesus' responds, "I am He." Jesus made this explicit declaration, of which we are wise to consider.

Since God foretold of sending a Messiah, Jesus declares it is He, and we have no other prospects, we must weigh these facts. The truth will impact everyone's future in whatever decision each person makes.

Jesus also spoke about people believing because of wonders they see. In the previous chapter, people didn't believe in spite of the wonders they saw.

Take a moment and consider what you base your beliefs upon. What might it take for you to believe in a Messiah, in Jesus, or to believe Jesus is God?

IS JESUS GOD?

➢ In this chapter, what does Jesus say about God, the Father?

_____
_____
_____
_____
_____
_____
_____

➢ In this chapter, what I AM declaration does Jesus make about who He is and what He has to offer us?

_____
_____
_____
_____
_____
_____
_____

WHAT DO YOU THINK?

➢ What was it that convinced people Jesus is the Messiah in this chapter?

_____
_____
_____
_____
_____
_____
_____

➤ In this chapter, Jesus plainly says He is the Messiah called Christ. What helps you believe or causes you to be uncertain about whether Jesus is actually the Messiah?

___

➤ What kinds of signs and wonders do you think people would actually believe in today's skeptical Society?

___

➤ What evidence exists that the spiritual realm has authority over the physical realm?

___

➤ What exactly is the gift of God, which Jesus gives to those who ask Him for it?

___

➢ How do you perceive The Living Water, of which Christ speaks? What do you think The Living Water is, and what could it do for you in your life?

➢ What is the food Jesus speaks of eating, and how does it sustain Him? In what ways can you reap God's harvest, and how can it sustain you?

➢ What does it mean to worship God in spirit and truth?

CHAPTER 5

After these things, there was a feast of the Jews, and Jesus went up to Jerusalem. Now in Jerusalem by the sheep gate, there is a pool, which is called in Hebrew, "Bethesda", having five porches. In these lay a great multitude of those who were sick, blind, lame, or paralyzed, waiting for the moving of the water; for an angel went down at certain times into the pool and stirred up the water. Whoever stepped in first after the stirring of the water was healed of whatever disease he had.

A certain man was there who had been sick for thirty-eight years. When Jesus saw him lying there, and knew that he had been sick for a long time, he asked him, *"Do you want to be made well?"*

The sick man answered him, "Sir, I have

no one to put me into the pool when the water is stirred up, but while I'm coming, another steps down before me."

Jesus said to him, *"Arise, take up your mat, and walk."*

Immediately, the man was made well, and took up his mat and walked.

Now it was the Sabbath on that day. So the Jews said to him who was cured, "It is the Sabbath. It is not lawful for you to carry the mat."

He answered them, "He who made me well said to me, 'Take up your mat and walk.'"

Then they asked him, "Who is the man who said to you, *'Take up your mat and walk'?"*

But he who was healed didn't know who it was, for Jesus had withdrawn, a crowd being in the place.

Afterward Jesus found him in the temple, and said to him, *"Behold, you are made well. Sin no more, so that nothing worse happens to you."*

The man went away, and told the Jews that it was Jesus who had made him well. For this cause the Jews persecuted Jesus, and sought to kill him, because he did these things on the Sabbath. But Jesus answered them, *"My Father is still working, so I am working, too."* For this cause therefore the Jews sought all the more to kill him, because he not only broke the Sabbath, but also called God his own Father, making himself equal with God.

Jesus therefore answered them, *"**Most certainly**, I tell you, the Son can do nothing of himself, but what he sees the Father doing. For whatever things he does, these the Son also does likewise. For the Father has affection for the Son, and shows him all things that he himself does. He will show him greater works than these, that you may marvel. For as the Father raises the dead and gives them life, even so the Son also gives life to whom he desires. For the Father judges no one, but he has given all judgment to the Son, that all may honor the Son, even as they honor the Father. He who doesn't honor the Son doesn't honor the Father who sent him.*

*"**Most certainly** I tell you, he who hears my word and **believes** him who sent me has eternal life, and doesn't come into judgment, but has passed out of death into life. **Most certainly** I tell you, the hour comes, and now is, when the dead will hear the Son of God's voice; and those who hear will live. For as the Father has life in himself, even so he gave to the Son also to have life in himself. He also gave him authority to execute judgment, because he is a son of man. Don't marvel at this, for the hour comes in which all who are in the tombs will hear his voice, and will come out; those who have done good, to the resurrection of life; and those who have done evil, to the resurrection of judgment. I can of myself do nothing. As I hear, I judge, and my judgment is righteous; because I don't seek my own will, but the will of my Father who sent me.*

"If I testify about myself, my witness

*is not valid. It is another who testifies about me. I know that the testimony which he testifies about me is true. You have sent to John, and he has testified to the truth. But the testimony which I receive is not from man. However, I say these things that you may be saved. He was the burning and shining lamp, and you were willing to rejoice for a while in his light. But the testimony which I have is greater than that of John, for the works which the Father gave me to accomplish, the very works that I do, testify about me, that the Father has sent me. The Father himself, who sent me, has testified about me. You have neither heard his voice at any time, nor seen his form. You don't have his word living in you, because you don't **believe** him whom he sent.*

*"You search the Scriptures, because you think that in them you have eternal life; and these are they which testify about me. Yet you will not come to me, that you may have life. I don't receive glory from men. But I know you, that you don't have God's love in yourselves. I have come in my Father's name, and you don't receive me. If another comes in his own name, you will receive him. How can you **believe**, who receive glory from one another, and you don't seek the glory that comes from the only God?*

*"Don't think that I will accuse you to the Father. There is one who accuses you, even Moses, on whom you have set your hope. For if you **believed** Moses, you would **believe** me; for he wrote about me. But if you don't **believe** his writings, how will you **believe** my words?"*

GOD AND JESUS REVELATIONS

In this chapter, the Jewish people get angry because Jesus "called God His own father, making Himself equal with God." Jesus also talks a lot about doing the work of His Father and the responsibilities God gave Jesus. There is a lot of information about Jesus and God, as Father and Son in this chapter.

Again we see Jesus has power over life and death, like God. People who believe in Jesus also believe what Jesus said. Those who don't believe Jesus or Moses don't believe what God said long ago as shared in the Old Testament. The Muslim and Jewish religions have the Old Testament in common with Christianity. Thus, people in the major religions have to decide whether they believe God's Word about a Messiah.

Each person who learns about Jesus has to decide whether they think He's telling the truth. Consider, for your own decision making, what impacts your beliefs about Jesus? What impacts your beliefs about God and the ancient scriptures about the Messiah?

IS JESUS GOD?

➢ In this chapter, what does Jesus say about God, the Father?

___

➢ In this chapter, what declarations does Jesus make about Himself?

___

WHAT DO YOU THINK?

➢ What three things does Jesus tell us are "most certain" in this chapter? Why are these certainties important for us in understanding who is Jesus?

➢ What does Jesus say about believing in Him in this chapter? Do you believe Him? Why or why not?

➢ What makes it difficult for people to believe Jesus is God's Son, and Jesus is equal to God?

➢ In what ways are Jesus and God the Father the same and different, as described by Jesus?

_____
_____
_____
_____
_____
_____
_____
_____

➢ Based on what Jesus says in this chapter, in what ways do you see Jesus and God as one deity versus being separate as Father and Son?

_____
_____
_____
_____
_____
_____
_____
_____

➢ Why does it matter who you think Jesus is?

_____
_____
_____
_____
_____
_____
_____
_____

➤ Jesus says John the Baptist, Jesus's works, God the Father, Moses, and the scriptures have all testified Jesus is who He says He is. Based on the testimonies you've heard so far, what would you say about who is Jesus?

➤ In what ways do our sins cause bad things to happen to us?

➤ If Jesus is God's Son, why is it dishonoring to God when people don't believe Jesus and ignore Him?

CHAPTER 6

After these things, Jesus went away to the other side of the sea of Galilee, which is also called the Sea of Tiberias. A great multitude followed him, because they saw his signs which he did on those who were sick. Jesus went up into the mountain, and he sat there with his disciples. Now the Passover, the feast of the Jews, was at hand. Jesus therefore lifting up his eyes, and seeing that a great multitude was coming to him, said to Philip, *"Where are we to buy bread, that these may eat?"* He said this to test him, for he himself knew what he would do.

Philip answered him, "Two hundred denarii worth of bread is not sufficient for them, that every one of them may receive a little."

One of his disciples, Andrew, Simon Peter's brother, said to him, "There is a boy here who has five barley loaves and two fish, but what are these among so many?" Jesus said, *"Have the people sit down."* Now there was much grass in that place. So the men sat down, in number about five thousand. Jesus took the loaves; and having given thanks, he distributed to the disciples, and the disciples to those who were sitting down; likewise also of the fish as much as they desired.

When they were filled, he said to his disciples, *"Gather up the broken pieces which are left over, that nothing be lost."* So they gathered them up, and filled twelve baskets with broken pieces from the five barley loaves, which were left over by those who had eaten.

When therefore the people saw the sign which Jesus did, they said, "This is truly the prophet who comes into the **world**." Jesus therefore, perceiving that they were about to come and take him by force to make him king, withdrew again to the mountain by himself.

When evening came, his disciples went down to the sea. They entered into the boat, and were going over the sea to Capernaum. It was now dark, and Jesus had not come to them. The sea was tossed by a great wind blowing. When therefore they had rowed about twenty-five or thirty stadia, they saw Jesus walking on the sea, and drawing near to the boat; and they were afraid. But he said to them, *"It is I. Don't be afraid."* They were willing therefore to receive him into the boat.

Immediately the boat was at the land where they were going.

On the next day, the multitude that stood on the other side of the sea saw that there was no other boat there, except the one in which his disciples had embarked, and that Jesus hadn't entered with his disciples into the boat, but his disciples had gone away alone. However boats from Tiberias came near to the place where they ate the bread after the Lord had given thanks. When the multitude therefore saw that Jesus wasn't there, nor his disciples, they themselves got into the boats, and came to Capernaum, seeking Jesus. When they found him on the other side of the sea, they asked him, "Rabbi, when did you come here?"

Jesus answered them, *"**Most certainly** I tell you, you seek me, not because you saw signs, but because you ate of the loaves, and were filled. Don't work for the food which perishes, but for the food which remains to eternal life, which the Son of Man will give to you. For God the Father has sealed him."*

They said therefore to him, "What must we do, that we may work the works of God?"

Jesus answered them, *"This is the work of God, that you **believe** in him whom he has sent."*

They said therefore to him, "What then do you do for a sign, that we may see and **believe** you? What work do you do? Our fathers ate the manna in the wilderness. As it is written, 'He gave them bread out of heaven to eat.' "

Jesus therefore said to them, "**Most certainly**, I tell you, it wasn't Moses who gave you the bread out of heaven, but my Father gives you the true bread out of heaven. For the bread of God is that which comes down out of heaven, and gives life to the **world**."

They said therefore to him, "Lord, always give us this bread."

Jesus said to them, "**I am the bread of life**. Whoever comes to me will not be hungry, and whoever **believes** in me will never be thirsty. But I told you that you have seen me, and yet you don't **believe**. All those whom the Father gives me will come to me. He who comes to me I will in no way throw out. For I have come down from heaven, not to do my own will, but the will of him who sent me. This is the will of my Father who sent me, that of all he has given to me I should lose nothing, but should raise him up at the last day. This is the will of the one who sent me, that everyone who sees the Son, and **believes** in him, should have eternal life; and I will raise him up at the last day."

The Jews therefore murmured concerning him, because he said, "**I am the bread which came down out of heaven**." They said, "Isn't this Jesus, the son of Joseph, whose father and mother we know? How then does he say, 'I have come down out of heaven?' "

Therefore Jesus answered them, "Don't murmur among yourselves. No one can *come to me unless the Father who sent me draws him, and I will raise him up in the last day. It is written in the prophets, 'They will all be taught by God.' Therefore everyone who hears from the Father and has learned, comes to me. Not that anyone has seen the Father, except he who is from God. He has seen the Father.* **Most certainly**, *I tell you, he who* **believes** *in me has eternal life.* **I am the bread of life**. *Your fathers ate the manna in the wilderness and they died. This is the bread which comes down out of heaven, that anyone may eat of it and not die.* **I am the living bread which came down out of heaven**. *If anyone eats of this bread, he will live forever. Yes, the bread which I will give for the life of the* **world** *is my flesh."*

The Jews therefore contended with one another, saying, "How can this man give us his flesh to eat?"

Jesus therefore said to them, "**Most certainly** *I tell you, unless you eat the flesh of the Son of Man and drink his blood, you don't have life in yourselves. He who eats my flesh and drinks my blood has eternal life, and I will raise him up at the last day. For my flesh is food indeed, and my blood is drink indeed. He who eats my flesh and drinks my blood lives in me, and I in him. As the living Father sent me, and I live because of the Father; so he who feeds on me, he will also live because of me. This is the bread which came down out of heaven—not as our fathers ate the* *manna, and died. He who eats this bread will live forever.*" He said these things in the synagogue, as he taught in Capernaum.

Therefore many of his disciples, when they heard this, said, "This is a hard saying! Who can listen to it?"

But Jesus knowing in himself that his disciples murmured at this, said to them, *"Does this cause you to stumble? Then what if you would see the Son of Man ascending to where he was before? It is the spirit who gives life. The flesh profits nothing. The words that I speak to you are spirit, and are life. But there are some of you who don't **believe**.*" For Jesus knew from the beginning who they were who didn't **believe**, and who it was who would betray him. He said, *"For this cause I have said to you that no one can come to me, unless it is given to him by my Father."*

At this, many of his disciples went back, and walked no more with him. Jesus said therefore to the twelve, *"You don't also want to go away, do you?"*

Simon Peter answered him, "Lord, to whom would we go? You have the words of eternal life. We have come to **believe** and know that you are the Christ, the Son of the living God."

Jesus answered them, *"Didn't I choose you, the twelve, and one of you is a devil?"* Now he spoke of Judas, the son of Simon Iscariot, for it was he who would betray him, being one of the twelve.

GOD AND JESUS REVELATIONS

Many people want to know what the will of God is for their lives. Their thoughts are often based on a desire to know what kind of work God desires them to do. This chapter clearly states what is the work of God for us. God's work is that you believe in Him whom He sent. In other words, the work God wants us to do is to believe Jesus!

How do we set about completing this work of God? You are completing God's work by completing this Bible study! Getting to know who Jesus is and what He taught brings you closer to God. That's because you can't believe Jesus if you don't know what He said. So take comfort, you are working on God's work right this minute!

IS JESUS GOD?

➢ In this chapter, what does Jesus say about God, the Father?

_____
_____
_____
_____
_____
_____
_____
_____
_____

➢ In this chapter, what I AM declaration does Jesus make? What other declarations does He make about Himself?

_____
_____
_____
_____
_____
_____
_____
_____
_____

WHAT DO YOU THINK?

➢ What four things does Jesus say are "most certain" in this chapter? What does Jesus say you have, if you believe in Him?

➢ Jesus says He is life to the world twice in this chapter. In what ways do you think Jesus gives life to the world and you besides giving eternal life?

➢ Jesus says He lives because of the Father. God the Father sent Jesus, and no one comes to Jesus unless God the Father, draws them near. What kind of relationship hierarchy does this show in the relationships between you, Jesus, and God?

➤ Jesus says, "I am the bread of the life, which gives life to the world." In what ways do you see Jesus gives life to the world?

___

➤ Symbolically, what do you think He means when Jesus says we must eat His flesh, drink His blood, and feed on Him?

___

➤ What kind of things do you think Jesus meant we should work for when He said, "Don't work for food which perishes, but for the food which remains to eternal life"?

___

➤ According to Jesus, in this chapter, what is the main work of God that we must do? What is God's clearly stated will?

CHAPTER 7

After these things, Jesus was walking in Galilee, for he wouldn't walk in Judea, because the Jews sought to kill him. Now the feast of the Jews, the Feast of Booths, was at hand. His brothers therefore said to him, "Depart from here and go into Judea, that your disciples also may see your works which you do. For no one does anything in secret while he seeks to be known openly. If you do these things, reveal yourself to the **world**." For even his brothers didn't **believe** in him.

Jesus therefore said to them, *"My time has not yet come, but your time is always ready. The* **world** *can't hate you, but it hates me, because I testify about it, that its works are evil. You go up to the feast. I am not yet going up to this* *feast, because my time is not yet fulfilled.*"

Having said these things to them, he stayed in Galilee. But when his brothers had gone up to the feast, then he also went up, not publicly, but as it were in secret. The Jews therefore sought him at the feast, and said, "Where is he?"

There was much murmuring among the multitudes concerning Jesus. Some said, "He is a good man." Others said, "Not so, but he leads the multitude astray." Yet no one spoke openly of him for fear of the Jews. But when it was now the middle of the feast, Jesus went up into the temple and taught. The Jews therefore marveled, saying, "How does this man know letters, having never been educated?"

Jesus therefore answered them, *"My teaching is not mine, but his who sent me. If anyone desires to do his will, he will know about the teaching, whether it is from God, or if I am speaking from myself. He who speaks from himself seeks his own glory, but he who seeks the glory of him who sent him is true, and no unrighteousness is in him. Didn't Moses give you the law, and yet none of you keeps the law? Why do you seek to kill me?"*

The multitude answered, "You have a demon! Who seeks to kill you?"

Jesus answered them, *"I did one work and you all marvel because of it. Moses has given you circumcision (not that it is of Moses, but of the fathers), and on the Sabbath you circumcise a boy. If a boy receives circumcision on the Sabbath, that the law of Moses may not be broken, are you angry with me, because I made a man completely healthy on the Sabbath? Don't judge according to appearance, but judge righteous judgment."*

Therefore some of them of Jerusalem said, "Isn't this he whom they seek to kill? Behold, he speaks openly, and they say nothing to him. Can it be that the rulers indeed know that this is truly the Christ? However we know where this man comes from, but when the Christ comes, no one will know where he comes from."

Jesus therefore cried out in the temple, teaching and saying, *"You both know me, and know where I am from. I have not come of myself, but he who sent me is true, whom you don't know. I know him, because* **I am from him**, *and he sent me."*

They sought therefore to take him; but no one laid a hand on him, because his hour had not yet come. But of the multitude, many **believed** in him. They said, "When the Christ comes, he won't do more signs than those which this man has done, will he?" The Pharisees heard the multitude murmuring these things concerning him, and the chief priests and the Pharisees sent officers to arrest him.

Then Jesus said, *"I will be with you a little while longer, then I go to him who sent me. You will seek me, and won't find me. You can't come where I am."*

The Jews therefore said among

themselves, "Where will this man go that we won't find him? Will he go to the Dispersion among the Greeks, and teach the Greeks?

What is this word that he said, *'You will seek me, and won't find me;'* and *'Where I am, you can't come'?"*

Now on the last and greatest day of the feast, Jesus stood and cried out, *"If anyone is thirsty, let him come to me and drink! He who **believes** in me, as the Scripture has said, from within him will flow rivers of living water."* But he said this about the Spirit, which those **believing** in him were to receive. For the Holy Spirit was not yet given, because Jesus wasn't yet glorified.

Many of the multitude therefore, when they heard these words, said, "This is truly the prophet." Others said, "This is the Christ." But some said, "What, does the Christ come out of Galilee? Hasn't the Scripture said that the Christ comes of the offspring of David, and from Bethlehem, the village where David was?"

So a division arose in the multitude because of him. Some of them would have arrested him, but no one laid hands on him. The officers therefore came to the chief priests and Pharisees, and they said to them, "Why didn't you bring him?"

The officers answered, "No man ever spoke like this man!"

The Pharisees therefore answered them, "You aren't also led astray, are you? Have any of the rulers **believed** in him, or of the Pharisees? But this multitude that doesn't know the law is cursed."

Nicodemus (he who came to him by night, being one of them) said to them, "Does our law judge a man, unless it first hears from him personally and knows what he does?"

They answered him, "Are you also from Galilee? Search, and see that no prophet has arisen out of Galilee."

Everyone went to his own house.

GOD AND JESUS REVELATIONS

In this chapter, did you notice the contention and constant desire of the Jewish leaders to get rid of Jesus? What is it in the hearts of men that makes them want to get rid of people they don't like or with whom they disagree?

Jesus speaks of God sending Him and returning to God. Jesus says He is from God. Consider for a moment what it means to be "from God." Consider also what it means when God sends someone, or when someone goes to God. We will all go to God at the end of our lives, whether we go for judgement or eternal life.

IS JESUS GOD?

➢ In this chapter, what does Jesus say about God, the Father?

➢ In this chapter, what I AM declaration does Jesus make and what else does He say about Himself?

WHAT DO YOU THINK?

➢ With what you know, why do you think some people believe Jesus is who He says He is, but others don't believe in Jesus at all?

➢ Why do you think a large number of people in the world hate Jesus and His ways?

➢ Do you think Jesus is a good man? Why or why not?

➢ What do you see in Jesus's teachings which clearly point to His teachings being from God?

➢ What criteria should we use to judge with righteous judgement, rather than according to appearance?

➢ How can we know if Jesus is truly the Christ? What are some resources from which we can pull reliable information?

➢ What do you think are the rivers of Living Water, which Jesus says will flow from those who believe in Him?

➢ The officers said no man ever spoke like Jesus! Describe how Jesus's speaking is different from other famous people you know.

CHAPTER 8

But Jesus went to the Mount of Olives. Now very early in the morning, he came again into the temple, and all the people came to him. He sat down and taught them. The scribes and the Pharisees brought a woman taken in adultery. Having set her in the middle, they told him, "Teacher, we found this woman in adultery, in the very act. Now in our law, Moses commanded us to stone such women. What then do you say about her?" They said this testing him, that they might have something to accuse him of.

But Jesus stooped down and wrote on the ground with his finger. But when they continued asking him, he looked up and said to them, *"He who is without sin among you, let him throw the first stone at her."* Again he stooped down and wrote on the ground with his finger.

They, when they heard it, being convicted by their conscience, went out one by one, beginning from the oldest, even to the last. Jesus was left alone with the woman where she was, in the middle. Jesus, standing up, saw her and said, *"Woman, where are your accusers? Did no one condemn you?"*

She said, "No one, Lord."

Jesus said, "Neither do I condemn you. Go your way. From now on, sin no more."

Again, therefore, Jesus spoke to them, saying, "**I am the light of the world**. He who follows me will not walk in the darkness, but will have the light of life."

The Pharisees therefore said to him, "You testify about yourself. Your testimony is not valid."

Jesus answered them, *"Even if I testify about myself, my testimony is true, for I know where I came from, and where I am going; but you don't know where I came from, or where I am going. You judge according to the flesh. I judge no one. Even if I do judge, my judgment is true, for* **I am not alone**, *but* **I am with the Father who sent me**. *It's also written in your law that the testimony of two people is valid. I am one who testifies about myself, and the Father who sent me testifies about me."*

They said therefore to him, "Where is your Father?"

Jesus answered, *"You know neither me nor my Father. If you knew me, you* would know my Father also." Jesus spoke these words in the treasury, as he taught in the temple. Yet no one arrested him, because his hour had not yet come. Jesus said therefore again to them, *"<u>I am going away</u>, and you will seek me, and you will die in your sins. Where I go, you can't come."*

The Jews therefore said, "Will he kill himself, because he says, 'Where I am going, you can't come'?"

He said to them, *"You are from beneath.* **I am from above***. You are of this* **world***.* **I am not of this world***. I said therefore to you that you will die in your sins; for unless you* **believe** *that* **I am he***, you will die in your sins."*

They said therefore to him, "Who are you?"

Jesus said to them, *"Just what I have been saying to you from the beginning. I have many things to speak and to judge concerning you. However he who sent me is true; and the things which I heard from him, these I say to the* **world***."*

They didn't understand that he spoke to them about the Father. Jesus therefore said to them, *"When you have lifted up the Son of Man, then you will know that* **I am he***, and I do nothing of myself, but as my Father taught me, I say these things. He who sent me is with me. The Father hasn't left me alone, for I always do the things that are pleasing to him."*

As he spoke these things, many **believed** in him. Jesus therefore said to *those Jews* who had **believed** him, *"If you remain in my word, then you are truly my disciples. You will know the truth, and the truth will make you free."*

They answered him, "We are Abraham's offspring, and have never been in bondage to anyone. How do you say, 'You will be made free'?"

Jesus answered them, **"Most certainly** *I tell you, everyone who commits sin is the bondservant of sin. A bondservant doesn't live in the house forever. A son remains forever. If therefore the Son makes you free, you will be free indeed. I know that you are Abraham's offspring, yet you seek to kill me, because my word finds no place in you. I say the things which I have seen with my Father; and you also do the things which you have seen with your father."*

They answered him, "Our father is Abraham."

Jesus said to them, *"If you were Abraham's children, you would do the works of Abraham. But now you seek to kill me, a man who has told you the truth which I heard from God. Abraham didn't do this. You do the works of your father."*

They said to him, "We were not born of sexual immorality. We have one Father, God."

Therefore Jesus said to them, *"If God were your father, you would love me, for I came out and have come from God. For I haven't come of myself, but he sent me. Why don't you understand my* *speech? Because you can't hear my word. You are of your father, the devil, and you want to do the desires of your father. He was a murderer from the beginning, and doesn't stand in the truth, because there is no truth in him. When he speaks a lie, he speaks on his own; for he is a liar, and the father of lies. But because I tell the truth, you don't **believe** me. Which of you convicts me of sin? If I tell the truth, why do you not **believe** me? He who is of God hears the words of God. For this cause you don't hear, because you are not of God."*

Then the Jews answered him, "Don't we say well that you are a Samaritan, and have a demon?"

Jesus answered, *"I don't have a demon, but I honor my Father and you dishonor me. But I don't seek my own glory. There is one who seeks and judges. **Most certainly**, I tell you, if a person keeps my word, he will never see death."*

Then the Jews said to him, "Now we know that you have a demon. Abraham died, as did the prophets; and you say, 'If a man keeps my word, he will never taste of death.' Are you greater than our father, Abraham, who died? The prophets died. Who do you make yourself out to be?"

Jesus answered, *"If I glorify myself, my glory is nothing. It is my Father who glorifies me, of whom you say that he is our God. You have not known him, but I know him. If I said, 'I don't know him,' I would be like you, a liar. But I know him and keep his word. Your father Abraham rejoiced to see my day. He saw it, and was glad."*

The Jews therefore said to him, "You are not yet fifty years old! Have you seen Abraham?"

Jesus said to them, ***"Most certainly**, I tell you, before Abraham came into existence, **I AM**."*

Therefore they took up stones to throw at him, but Jesus was hidden, and went out of the temple, having gone through the middle of them, and so passed by.

GOD AND JESUS REVELATIONS

In this chapter, Jesus said He is not alone, but He is with the Father who sent Him. This statement indicates Jesus is not alone. If God is with Jesus, then God is spiritually present with, within, or a as Jesus. Jesus says His Father testifies about Him. God testifed about Jesus in the Old Testament scriptures. Those scriptures still testify about Jesus today.

The Old Testament scriptures quoted below give insights into God and Jesus's relationship. I have also included a verse from The Book of Revelation for you, which is in the New Testament.

Isaiah 44:6 says there is only ONE God:

"This is what The Lord, the King of Israel, and his Redeemer, The Lord of Armies, says: 'I am the first, and I am the last; and besides me there is no God.'"

The ONE God is the only Savior. Isaiah 43:11: "I myself am The Lord. Besides me, there is no savior."

Yet, God speaks in plurality about making man in "our" image in Genesis 1:26:

"God said, 'Let's make man in our image, after our likeness.'" This is the image of the Father, Son, and Holy Spirit as a Trinity. They are three persons.

In Psalm 2, in verses 7 & 12 in particular, we see the Son is separate from the Father.

"I will tell of the decree: The Lord said to me, "You are my son. Today I have become your father." "Give sincere homage to the Son, lest He be angry, and you perish on the way, for His wrath will soon be kindled. Blessed are all those who take refuge in Him."

Exodus 3:14 is important because God tells Moses to call God, "I AM." "God said to Moses, 'I AM WHO I AM,' and he said, 'You shall tell the children of Israel this: 'I AM has sent me to you.'"" In this chapter, Jesus says, "Before Moses, I AM." Thus, both God and Jesus refer to themselves as, "I AM."

Revelation 1:17-18 speaks of Jesus who "was and is the first and last, who was dead, but lives. Revelation 1 says, "He laid His right hand on me, saying, 'Don't be afraid. I am the first and the last, and the Living One. I was dead, and behold, I am alive forever and ever. Amen. I have the keys of Death and of Hades.'"

The ancient scriptures and Jesus Himself says there's only one God. Yet, there's also a Son who judges and takes away the sins of the world, who is the first and last.

IS JESUS GOD?

➢ In this chapter, what does Jesus say about God, the Father?

_____
_____
_____
_____
_____
_____
_____
_____
_____

➢ In this chapter, what does Jesus's "I AM" declaration mean to you? What else does He say about Himself?

_____
_____
_____
_____
_____
_____
_____
_____

WHAT DO YOU THINK?

➤ What three things does Jesus tell us are "most certain" in this chapter? What aspects of these certainties do you struggle with, if any?

➤ How do people's lives look different when they walk in the light, versus walk in darkness, within their souls?

➤ What important concept(s) about His judgment of people does Jesus teach in this chapter? In what ways do you struggle with these judgment truths?

➢ In what ways do you see Jesus is the light of the world?

➢ Jesus says, "You are of this world, I am not of this world." In what ways does this critical difference impact you in living your life and in your relationship with Jesus?

➢ How does knowing the truth, as Jesus taught us, set us free?

➢ What message(s) do you think Jesus is trying to convey to us when he says, "Before Abraham came into existence, I AM"?

➢ What does it mean to you to be of God? What impact do you think it will have on your life, if you are really able to understand and believe the Word of God?

CHAPTER 9

As he passed by, he saw a man blind from birth. His disciples asked him, "Rabbi, who sinned, this man or his parents, that he was born blind?"

Jesus answered, *"This man didn't sin, nor did his parents; but, that the works of God might be revealed in him. I must work the works of him who sent me while it is day. The night is coming, when no one can work. While I am in the **world**, **I am the light of the world**."*

When he had said this, he spat on the ground, made mud with the saliva, anointed the blind man's eyes with the mud, and said to him, *"Go, wash in the pool of Siloam"* (which means "Sent"). So he went away, washed, and came back seeing. The neighbors therefore, and those who saw that he was blind before, said, "Isn't this he who sat and begged?" Others were saying, "It is he." Still others were saying, "He looks like him."

He said, "I am he." They therefore were asking him, "How were your eyes opened?"

He answered, "A man called Jesus made mud, anointed my eyes, and said to me, *'Go to the pool of Siloam and wash.'* So I went away and washed, and I received sight."

Then they asked him, "Where is he?" He said, "I don't know."

They brought him who had been blind to the Pharisees. It was a Sabbath when Jesus made the mud and opened his eyes. Again therefore the Pharisees also asked him how he received his sight. He said to them, "He put mud on my eyes, I washed, and I see."

Some therefore of the Pharisees said, "This man is not from God, because he doesn't keep the Sabbath." Others said, "How can a man who is a sinner do such signs?" There was division among them. Therefore they asked the blind man again, "What do you say about him, because he opened your eyes?"

He said, "He is a prophet."

The Jews therefore didn't **believe** concerning him, that he had been blind, and had received his sight, until they called the parents of him who had received his sight, and asked them, "Is this your son, whom you say was born blind? How then does he now see?"

His parents answered them, "We know that this is our son, and that he was born blind; but how he now sees, we don't know; or who opened his eyes, we don't know. He is of age. Ask him. He will speak for himself."

His parents said these things because they feared the Jews; for the Jews had already agreed that if any man would confess him as Christ, he would be put out of the synagogue. Therefore his parents said, "He is of age. Ask him."

So they called the man who was blind a second time, and said to him, "Give glory to God. We know that this man is a sinner."

He therefore answered, "I don't know if he is a sinner. One thing I do know: that though I was blind, now I see." They said to him again, "What did he do to you? How did he open your eyes?"

He answered them, "I told you already, and you didn't listen. Why do you want to hear it again? You don't also want to become his disciples, do you?"

They insulted him and said, "You are his disciple, but we are disciples of Moses. We know that God has spoken to Moses. But as for this man, we don't know where he comes from."

The man answered them, "How amazing! You don't know where he comes from, yet he opened my eyes. We know that God doesn't listen to sinners, but if anyone is a worshiper of God, and does his will, he listens to him.

Since the **world** began it has never been heard of that anyone opened the eyes of someone born blind. If this man were not from God, he could do nothing."

They answered him, "You were altogether born in sins, and do you teach us?" Then they threw him out.

Jesus heard that they had thrown him out, and finding him, he said, *"Do you **believe** in the Son of God?"*

He answered, "Who is he, Lord, that I may **believe** in him?"

Jesus said to him, *"You have both seen him, and it is he who speaks with you."*

He said, "Lord, I **believe**!" and he worshiped him.

Jesus said, *"I came into this **world** for judgment, that those who don't see may see; and that those who see may become blind."*

Those of the Pharisees who were with him heard these things, and said to him, "Are we also blind?"

Jesus said to them, *"If you were blind, you would have no sin; but now you say, 'We see.' Therefore your sin remains."*

GOD AND JESUS REVELATIONS

The man who was born blind serves God's purpose of revealing God's work. Giving sight to the blind man was one of God's chosen ways of evidencing Jesus's power to the world. Jesus said, "I came into this world for judgment, that those who don't see may see, and that those who see may become blind."

We have to consider whether our eyes are open. Are we looking for evidence of God's power in the world? Our eyes have to be open to see if Jesus is real and God exists.

God provided a way for us to see His power, thereby inviting us to see Jesus as the Savior with God-given powers. Some people do not see the power of God, because they aren't focused on what God is doing. Instead, skeptical people focus on judging the actions of people, and they hold people's actions against God. Unfortunately, they are judging incorrectly!

John says the Jews predetermined this man (Jesus) is a sinner. Thus, they weren't looking for God's means for the miracles carried out by Jesus. They were judging Jesus, rather than experiencing awe. They were blind to the miracle right before their eyes.

Whether we see God through Jesus, as Jesus, or Jesus as God's Son, we have to be looking for God to see Him in Jesus. We have to be looking for God's presence in our own lives to be able to see Him. Take a minute to look around and consider: Where do you see God at work in your life or the lives of people you know?

IS JESUS GOD?
- In this chapter, what does Jesus say about God, the Father?

\
\
\
\
\
\
\
\

- In this chapter, what I AM declaration does Jesus make, and what else does He say about Himself?

\
\
\
\
\
\
\

WHAT DO YOU THINK?
- Based on your own knowledge of the Bible and what Jesus says in this chapter, what are some reasons bad things happen to good people?

\
\
\
\
\
\
\

➢ What point do you think Jesus is trying to make in performing so many miracles on the Sabbath day?

➢ If Jesus is the light of the world while He's in the world, what happens if Jesus is no longer in the world?

➢ What causes divisions among people who believe in Jesus and those who don't believe in Jesus?

- The Jews pre-determined they would not believe in Jesus Christ as the Messiah. What makes people unwilling to examine Jesus's life, character, and teachings before deciding who they think Jesus is?

- In this chapter, it says, "If anyone is a worshipper of God and does His will, God listens to that person." Based on this statement, do you think God listens to you? Why or why not? What might you want to change in your relationship with God?

- Jesus reveals the truth to those who are blind to it, and hides the truth from those who arrogantly think they know it. How and where do you see this kind of spiritual blindness affecting people in the world today?

➢ Since the time of Jesus's death, what evidence do we have that Jesus is the son of God and the light of the world? If Jesus lied about who He is, what would be different in the world today?

CHAPTER 10

"**Most certainly**, I tell you, one who doesn't enter by the door into the sheep fold, but climbs up some other way, is a thief and a robber. But one who enters in by the door is the shepherd of the sheep. The gatekeeper opens the gate for him, and the sheep listen to his voice. He calls his own sheep by name, and leads them out. Whenever he brings out his own sheep, he goes before them, and the sheep follow him, for they know his voice. They will by no means follow a stranger, but will flee from him; for they don't know the voice of strangers." Jesus spoke this parable to them, but they didn't understand what he was telling them.

Jesus therefore said to them again,

"**Most certainly**, I tell you, **I am the sheep's door**. All who came before me are thieves and robbers, but the sheep didn't listen to them. **I am the door**. If anyone enters in by me, he will be saved, and will go in and go out, and will find pasture. The thief only comes to steal, kill, and destroy. I came that they may have life, and may have it abundantly. **I am the good shepherd**. The good shepherd lays down his life for the sheep. He who is a hired hand, and not a shepherd, who doesn't own the sheep, sees the wolf coming, leaves the sheep, and flees. The wolf snatches the sheep, and scatters them. The hired hand flees because he is a hired hand, and doesn't care for the sheep. **I am the good shepherd**. I know my own, and I'm known by my own; even as the Father knows me, and I know the Father. I lay down my life for the sheep. I have other sheep, which are not of this fold. I must bring them also, and they will hear my voice. They will become one flock with one shepherd. Therefore the Father loves me, because I lay down my life, that I may take it again. No one takes it away from me, but I lay it down by myself. I have power to lay it down, and I have power to take it again. I received this commandment from my Father."

Therefore a division arose again among the Jews because of these words. Many of them said, "He has a demon, and is insane! Why do you listen to him?" Others said,

"These are not the sayings of one possessed by a demon. It isn't possible for a demon to open the eyes of the blind, is it?"

It was the Feast of the Dedication at Jerusalem. It was winter, and Jesus was walking in the temple, in Solomon's porch. The Jews therefore came around him and said to him, "How long will you hold us in suspense? If you are the Christ, tell us plainly."

Jesus answered them, *"I told you, and you don't **believe**. The works that I do in my Father's name, these testify about me. But you don't **believe**, because you are not of my sheep, as I told you. My sheep hear my voice, and I know them, and they follow me. I give eternal life to them. They will never perish, and no one will snatch them out of my hand. My Father who has given them to me is greater than all. No one is able to snatch them out of my Father's hand. I and the Father are one."*

Therefore Jews took up stones again to stone him. Jesus answered them, *"I have shown you many good works from my Father. For which of those works do you stone me?"*

The Jews answered him, "We don't stone you for a good work, but for blasphemy: because you, being a man, make yourself God."

Jesus answered them, *"Isn't it written in your law, 'I said, you are gods?' If he called them gods, to whom the word of God came (and the Scripture can't be broken), do you say of him whom the*

*Father sanctified and sent into the **world**, 'You blaspheme,' because I said, '**I am the Son of God**?' If I don't do the works of my Father, don't **believe** me. But if I do them, though you don't **believe** me, **believe** the works, that you may know and **believe** that the Father is in me, and I in the Father."*

They sought again to seize him, and he went out of their hand. He went away again beyond the Jordan into the place where John was baptizing at first, and he stayed there. Many came to him. They said, "John indeed did no sign, but everything that John said about this man is true." Many **believed** in him there.

GOD AND JESUS REVELATIONS

In this chapter, the shepherd is Jesus, and the Sheep are His followers. Those who follow Jesus know His voice. How do they know His voice? They learn to hear it by getting to know as much as they can about Jesus.

The best way I know to learn Jesus's voice is to study the Gospel books of Matthew, Mark, Luke, and John. The key is to focus on all Jesus says and does. When you get to know Jesus, you know the kinds of things He says and does. By becoming familiar with Jesus, you know the truths Jesus teaches and learn to discern the voice of God.

You are getting to know Jesus's voice in this study. The more you continue to study Jesus, the more clearly you'll hear and know His voice. Soon you will be able to see God the Father in Jesus. Everything about Jesus reflects God the Father.

IS JESUS GOD?

➢ In this chapter, what does Jesus say about God, the Father?

➤ What two I AM declarations does Jesus make about himself in this chapter? What other declarations does He make about Himself?

_____
_____
_____
_____
_____
_____
_____

WHAT DO YOU THINK?

➤ What two things does Jesus tell us are most certain in this chapter?

_____
_____
_____
_____
_____
_____
_____

➤ How do Jesus's I AM statements in this chapter convey the type of relationship we have with Jesus?

_____
_____
_____
_____
_____
_____
_____

➢ How can you discern the difference between Jesus's, God's, and the Holy Spirit's voices over other voices from which you should flee? What are your most reliable sources of information about what the voices of the Holy Trinity sound like?

___

➢ What was it like, or what do you think it will be like, when you first hear(d) Jesus's voice? Why do you want to hear God's voice? What makes you want to hear Him?

___

➢ What do you think Jesus means when He says, "I come that they may have life, and they may have it abundantly"? What does an abundant life look like for you?

___

- When Jesus said He is one with God, the Jews became angry because Jesus "made Himself God." What critical possibility were the Jews overlooking, and how can we keep from making similar mistakes in our judgments?

- In this chapter, Jesus explicitly states He and God the Father are one. What works and abilities have we seen, which demonstrate Jesus has the same abilities as God?

- What does it mean for God to be in Jesus and Jesus in God? How is this the same and different from Jesus being in us and us being in Jesus?

CHAPTER 11

Now a certain man was sick, Lazarus from Bethany, of the village of Mary and her sister, Martha. It was that Mary who had anointed the Lord with ointment and wiped his feet with her hair, whose brother, Lazarus, was sick. The sisters therefore sent to him, saying, "Lord, behold, he for whom you have great affection is sick." But when Jesus heard it, he said, *"This sickness is not to death, but for the glory of God, that God's Son may be glorified by it."* Now Jesus loved Martha, and her sister, and Lazarus. When therefore he heard that he was sick, he stayed two days in the place where he was. Then after this he said to the disciples, *"Let's go into Judea again."*

The disciples asked him, "Rabbi, the

Jews were just trying to stone you. Are you going there again?"

Jesus answered, *"Aren't there twelve hours of daylight? If a man walks in the day, he doesn't stumble, because he sees the light of this **world**. But if a man walks in the night, he stumbles, because the light isn't in him."*

He said these things, and after that, he said to them, *"Our friend, Lazarus, has fallen asleep, but I am going so that I may awake him out of sleep."*

The disciples therefore said, "Lord, if he has fallen asleep, he will recover."

Now Jesus had spoken of his death, but they thought that he spoke of taking rest in sleep. So Jesus said to them plainly then, *"Lazarus is dead. I am glad for your sakes that I was not there, so that you may **believe**. Nevertheless, let's go to him."*

Thomas therefore, who is called Didymus, said to his fellow disciples, "Let's go also, that we may die with him." So when Jesus came, he found that he had been in the tomb four days already. Now Bethany was near Jerusalem, about fifteen stadia away. Many of the Jews had joined the women around Martha and Mary, to console them concerning their brother.

Then when Martha heard that Jesus was coming, she went and met him, but Mary stayed in the house. Therefore Martha said to Jesus, "Lord, if you would have been here, my brother wouldn't have died. Even now I know that whatever you ask of God, God will give you."

Jesus said to her, *"Your brother will rise again."*

Martha said to him, "I know that he will rise again in the resurrection at the last day."

Jesus said to her, *"**I am the resurrection and the life**. He who **believes** in me will still live, even if he dies. Whoever lives and **believes** in me will never die. Do you **believe** this?"*

She said to him, "Yes, Lord. I have come to **believe** that you are the Christ, God's Son, he who comes into the **world**."

When she had said this, she went away and called Mary, her sister, secretly, saying, "The Teacher is here and is calling you."

When she heard this, she arose quickly and went to him. Now Jesus had not yet come into the village, but was in the place where Martha met him. Then the Jews who were with her in the house and were consoling her, when they saw Mary, that she rose up quickly and went out, followed her, saying, "She is going to the tomb to weep there." Therefore when Mary came to where Jesus was and saw him, she fell down at his feet, saying to him, "Lord, if you would have been here, my brother wouldn't have died."

When Jesus therefore saw her weeping, and the Jews weeping who came with her, he groaned in the spirit, and was troubled, and said, *"Where have you laid him?"*

They told him, "Lord, come and see."

Jesus wept.

The Jews therefore said, "See how much affection he had for him!" Some of them said, "Couldn't this man, who opened the eyes of him who was blind, have also kept this man from dying?"

Jesus therefore, again groaning in himself, came to the tomb. Now it was a cave, and a stone lay against it. Jesus said, *"Take away the stone."*

Martha, the sister of him who was dead, said to him, "Lord, by this time there is a stench, for he has been dead four days."

Jesus said to her, *"Didn't I tell you that if you **believed**, you would see God's glory?"*

So they took away the stone from the place where the dead man was lying. Jesus lifted up his eyes, and said, *"Father, I thank you that you listened to me. I know that you always listen to me, but because of the multitude standing around I said this, that they may **believe** that you sent me."*

When he had said this, he cried with a loud voice, *"Lazarus, come out!"*

He who was dead came out, bound hand and foot with wrappings, and his face was wrapped around with a cloth.

Jesus said to them, *"Free him, and let him go."*

Therefore many of the Jews who came to Mary and saw what Jesus did **believed** in him. But some of them went away to the Pharisees and told them the things which Jesus had done. The chief priests therefore and the Pharisees gathered a council, and said, "What are we doing? For this man does many signs. If we leave him alone like this, everyone will **believe** in him, and the Romans will come and take away both our place and our nation."

But a certain one of them, Caiaphas, being high priest that year, said to them, "You know nothing at all, nor do you consider that it is advantageous for us that one man should die for the people, and that the whole nation not perish." Now he didn't say this of himself, but being high priest that year, he prophesied that Jesus would die for the nation, and not for the nation only, but that he might also gather together into one the children of God who are scattered abroad. So from that day forward they took counsel that they might put him to death. Jesus therefore walked no more openly among the Jews, but departed from there into the country near the wilderness, to a city called Ephraim. He stayed there with his disciples.

Now the Passover of the Jews was at hand. Many went up from the country to Jerusalem before the Passover, to purify themselves. Then they sought for Jesus and spoke with one another as they stood in the temple, "What do you think—that he isn't coming to the feast at all?" Now the chief priests and the Pharisees had commanded that if anyone knew where he was, he should report it, that they might seize him.

GOD AND JESUS REVELATIONS

In this chapter, Jesus said He has power over illness, life and death. Jesus also demonstrates that power. Jesus said people would see "God's glory" when Jesus raised Lazarus from the dead. And they saw God's glory when Lazarus was resurrected.

Jesus states, "He who believes in me will still live, even if he dies. Whoever lives and believes in Me will never die." Whether you believe Jesus is actually God or not, Jesus has power over life and death.

IS JESUS GOD?

➤ In this chapter, what does Jesus say about God, the Father, especially about Him listening to Jesus? What is the importance of God, the Father, listening to Jesus?

➤ In this chapter, what I AM declaration does Jesus make and what else does He say about believing in Him?

WHAT DO YOU THINK?

➤ If you were to see God's glory, what would you expect or hope to see?

- What does Jesus mean when He says, "This sickness is not to death, but for the glory of God, that God's Son may be glorified in it," when referring to Lazarus's sickness? In what ways can you give God glory when you are sick?

- Why do you think Jesus wept when He knew He was about to raise Lazarus from the dead? Why do we weep for people who have died in Christ?

- This chapter says Jesus was again groaning in Himself. What kinds of things do you do, which you think might make Jesus groan? What can you do about those things?

- The Pharisees and chief priests were afraid they'd lose their power because of Jesus, so they wanted to kill Him. Why is Christianity similarly seen as a threat to strong, controlling regimes in the world today?

- In what ways does Jesus's resurrection of Lazarus demonstrate Jesus has the power of God at His command?

- What do you think it means when Jesus says He is the resurrection and the life?

- Do you think your belief is strong enough to see God's glory? Why or why not?

CHAPTER 12

Then six days before the Passover, Jesus came to Bethany, where Lazarus was, who had been dead, whom he raised from the dead. So they made him a supper there. Martha served, but Lazarus was one of those who sat at the table with him.

Therefore Mary took a pound of ointment of pure nard, very precious, and anointed Jesus's feet and wiped his feet with her hair. The house was filled with the fragrance of the ointment.

Then Judas Iscariot, Simon's son, one of his disciples, who would betray him, said, "Why wasn't this ointment sold for three hundred denarii, and given to the poor?"

Now he said this, not because he cared for the poor, but because he was a thief, and having the money box, used to steal what was put into it. But Jesus said,

"Leave her alone. She has kept this for the day of my burial. For you always have the poor with you, but you don't always have me."

A large crowd therefore of the Jews learned that he was there, and they came, not for Jesus' sake only, but that they might see Lazarus also, whom he had raised from the dead. But the chief priests conspired to put Lazarus to death also, because on account of him many of the Jews went away and **believed** in Jesus.

On the next day a great multitude had come to the feast. When they heard that Jesus was coming to Jerusalem, they took the branches of the palm trees and went out to meet him, and cried out, "Hosanna! Blessed is he who comes in the name of the Lord, the King of Israel!"

Jesus, having found a young donkey, sat on it. As it is written, "Don't be afraid, daughter of Zion. Behold, your King comes, sitting on a donkey's colt." His disciples didn't understand these things at first, but when Jesus was glorified, then they remembered that these things were written about him, and that they had done these things to him. The multitude therefore that was with him when he called Lazarus out of the tomb and raised him from the dead was testifying about it. For this cause also the multitude went and met him, because they heard that he had done this sign. The Pharisees therefore said among themselves, "See how you accomplish nothing. Behold, the world has gone after him."

Now there were certain Greeks among those that went up to worship at the feast.

These, therefore, came to Philip, who was from Bethsaida of Galilee, and asked him, saying, "Sir, we want to see Jesus." Philip came and told Andrew, and in turn, Andrew came with Philip, and they told Jesus.

Jesus answered them, *"The time has come for the Son of Man to be glorified.* **Most certainly** *I tell you, unless a grain of wheat falls into the earth and dies, it remains by itself alone. But if it dies, it bears much fruit. He who loves his life will lose it. He who hates his life in this* **world** *will keep it to eternal life. If anyone serves me, let him follow me. Where I am, there my servant will also be. If anyone serves me, the Father will honor him.*

"Now my soul is troubled. What shall I say? 'Father, save me from this time?' But I came to this time for this cause. Father, glorify your name!"

Then a voice came out of the sky, saying, *"I have both glorified it, and will glorify it again."*

Therefore the multitude who stood by and heard it said that it had thundered. Others said, "An angel has spoken to him."

Jesus answered, *"This voice hasn't come for my sake, but for your sakes. Now is the judgment of this* **world**. *Now the prince of this* **world** *will be cast out. And I, if I am lifted up from the earth, will draw all people to myself."* But he said this, signifying by what kind of death he should die.

The multitude answered him, "We have heard out of the law that the Christ remains forever. How do you say, *'The Son of Man must be lifted up?'* Who is this Son of Man?"

Jesus therefore said to them, *"Yet a little while the light is with you. Walk while you have the light, that darkness doesn't overtake you. He who walks in the darkness doesn't know where he is going. While you have the light,* **believe** *in the light, that you may become children of light."* Jesus said these things, and he departed and hid himself from them. But though he had done so many signs before them, yet they didn't **believe** in him, that the word of Isaiah the prophet might be fulfilled, which he spoke,

"Lord, who has **believed** our report?

To whom has the arm of the Lord been revealed?"

For this cause they couldn't **believe**, for Isaiah said again,

"He has blinded their eyes and he hardened their heart, lest they should see with their eyes, and perceive with their heart, and would turn, and I would heal them."

Isaiah said these things when he saw his glory, and spoke of him. Nevertheless even many of the rulers **believed** in him, but because of the Pharisees they didn't confess it, so that they wouldn't be put out of the synagogue, for they loved men's praise more than God's praise.

Jesus cried out and said, *"Whoever* ***believes*** *in me,* ***believes*** *not in me, but in him who sent me. He who sees me sees him who sent me. I have come as a* *light into the **world**, that whoever **believes** in me may not remain in the darkness. If anyone listens to my sayings, and doesn't **believe**, I don't judge him. For I came not to judge the **world**, but to save the **world**. He who rejects me, and doesn't receive my sayings, has one who judges him. The word that I spoke will judge him in the last day. For I spoke not from myself, but the Father who sent me, he gave me a commandment, what I should say, and what I should speak. I know that his commandment is eternal life. The things therefore which I speak, even as the Father has said to me, so I speak."*

GOD AND JESUS REVELATIONS

In this chapter, the chief priests want to put Lazarus and Jesus to death, so people won't believe in Jesus. The chief priests want to get rid of all evidence that Jesus is the Messiah. They refuse to examine the evidence or consider the possibility Jesus is the Messiah. They have blinders on, like many people today. They fail to examine Jesus before rejecting Him.

Jesus says He came to glorify God's name. Jesus is willing to go to His death, because He knows He will continue to live. He knows His resurrection will glorify God. Ultimately, Jesus' coming to Earth demonstrated God's power over death. It revealed to us there is spiritual life after death. Thus, we ought to consider whether Jesus Is God showing us eternal life exists.

IS JESUS GOD?

➢ In this chapter, what does Jesus say about those who believe in Him, and how does belief in Jesus relate to belief in God, the Father?

- In this chapter, what declarations does Jesus make using a metaphor to describe Himself?

WHAT DO YOU THINK?

- What evidence do we have that Satan is currently the prince of our world?

- In this chapter, for what specific reason does Jesus say He came into the world?

- How has Jesus's death brought forth a bounty of fruit in the world?

➢ If you believe Jesus is God, who came to show us there is eternal life, what impact does your belief have on your feelings about Jesus?

➢ What's inside a person's heart and soul, which makes him want to harm or kill people who challenge that person's wisdom or authority?

➢ What do you think makes people in the world, throughout the ages, desire Jesus?

➢ Why do most people prefer the praise of other people more than the praise of God?

➢ Jesus says, if anyone serves me, the Father will honor him. In what ways can you serve Jesus and God?

➢ To the best of your ability, describe how the forces of light and darkness affect people's relationships with God and each other.

➢ How can believing in and seeing the light (Jesus) help us live in the light?

CHAPTER 13

Now before the feast of the Passover, Jesus, knowing that his time had come that he would depart from this **world** to the Father, having loved his own who were in the **world**, he loved them to the end. During supper, the devil having already put into the heart of Judas Iscariot, Simon's son, to betray him, Jesus, knowing that the Father had given all things into his hands, and that he came from God, and was going to God, arose from supper, and laid aside his outer garments. He took a towel and wrapped a towel around his waist. Then he poured water into the basin, and began to wash the disciples' feet and to wipe them with the towel that was wrapped around him. Then he came to Simon Peter. He said to him, "Lord, do you wash my feet?"

Jesus answered him, *"You don't know what I am doing now, but you will understand later."*

Peter said to him, "You will never wash my feet!"

Jesus answered him, *"If I don't wash you, you have no part with me."*

Simon Peter said to him, "Lord, not my feet only, but also my hands and my head!"

Jesus said to him, *"Someone who has bathed only needs to have his feet washed, but is completely clean. You are clean, but not all of you."* For he knew him who would betray him, therefore he said, *"You are not all clean."*

So when he had washed their feet, put his outer garment back on, and sat down again, he said to them, *"Do you know what I have done to you? You call me, 'Teacher' and 'Lord.' You say so correctly, for so I am. If I then, the Lord and the Teacher, have washed your feet, you also ought to wash one another's feet. For I have given you an example, that you should also do as I have done to you.* **Most certainly** *I tell you, a servant is not greater than his lord, neither is one who is sent greater than he who sent him. If you know these things, blessed are you if you do them. I don't speak concerning all of you. I know whom I have chosen. But that the Scripture may be fulfilled, 'He who eats bread with me has lifted up his heel against me.' From now on, I tell you before it happens, that when it happens, you may* **believe** *that* **I am he.**

Most certainly I tell you, he who receives whomever I send, receives me; and he who receives me, receives him who sent me."

When Jesus had said this, he was troubled in spirit, and testified, *"Most certainly I tell you that one of you will betray me."*

The disciples looked at one another, perplexed about whom he spoke. One of his disciples, whom Jesus loved, was at the table, leaning against Jesus' breast. Simon Peter therefore beckoned to him, and said to him, "Tell us who it is of whom he speaks."

He, leaning back, as he was, on Jesus' breast, asked him, "Lord, who is it?"

Jesus therefore answered, *"It is he to whom I will give this piece of bread when I have dipped it."* So when he had dipped the piece of bread, he gave it to Judas, the son of Simon Iscariot. After the piece of bread, then Satan entered into him.

Then Jesus said to him, *"What you do, do quickly."*

Now nobody at the table knew why he said this to him. For some thought, because Judas had the money box, that Jesus said to him, "Buy what things we need for the feast," or that he should give something to the poor. Therefore having received that morsel, he went out immediately. It was night.

When he had gone out, Jesus said, *"Now the Son of Man has been glorified, and God has been glorified in him. If*

God has been glorified in him, God will also glorify him in himself, and he will glorify him immediately. Little children, I will be with you a little while longer. You will seek me, and as I said to the Jews, 'Where I am going, you can't come,' so now I tell you. A new commandment I give to you, that you love one another. Just as I have loved you, you also love one another. By this everyone will know that you are my disciples, if you have love for one another."

Simon Peter said to him, "Lord, where are you going?"

Jesus answered, *"Where I am going, you can't follow now, but you will follow afterwards."*

Peter said to him, "Lord, why can't I follow you now? I will lay down my life for you."

Jesus answered him, *"Will you lay down your life for me?* **Most certainly** *I tell you, the rooster won't crow until you have denied me three times."*

GOD AND JESUS REVELATIONS

In this chapter, Jesus says from this point onward, He will tell his disciples what will happen before it happens. Jesus pre-tells events to strengthen their belief in Him.

Jesus knew His death was coming. According to the first paragraph in this chapter, Jesus knew He was in control of everything. Even though He was completely in control, Jesus chose death and resurrection. Rather than stop His betrayer, His killers, or to prevent His death, Jesus chose to suffer, die and rise again.

Contemplate for a moment the greater benefit created by Jesus' death and resurrection. He could strike down the people who opposed Him. Instead, Jesus submitted to death to bring about a great outcome. Take a moment to think about the centuries long effect of Jesus's resurrection on the world.

What doors did Jesus open, and what opportunities did He create, by submitting to the people who opposed Him? Even in His dying, Jesus was acting as teacher and Lord. He was in control of everything, and prophesied everything that was to come.

IS JESUS GOD?

- In this chapter, what does Jesus say about God, the Father, and glorifying Him?

- In this chapter, what I AM declaration does Jesus make? What other declarations does He make about Himself and His role on earth?

WHAT DO YOU THINK?

- What does Jesus tell us is most certain in this chapter?

➢ What makes your heart and soul clean in Jesus's eyes?

➢ This chapter says God gave all things into Jesus's hands. Since all things were given into Jesus's hands, why do you think neither God nor Jesus simply made everyone believe in them, when they could open everyone's eyes and ears to the truth?

➢ Jesus says, "He who receives me, receives Him who sent me." In what ways does receiving Jesus equal receiving God the Father, and also the Holy Spirit?

➤ What are some ways you can serve other people, like Jesus served His disciples? Why is it important to serve others in a spirit of love?

➤ Jesus says he is both teacher and Lord. Is God, the Father, also our teacher and Lord? In these roles, how do you believe Jesus and God relate to each other, and to us?

➤ If Jesus has all things under His control, what separation or what difference do you believe exists between Jesus and God the Father?

➢ In what ways is God or has God been glorified in Jesus?

CHAPTER 14

"Don't let your heart be troubled. **Believe** in God. **Believe** also in me. In my Father's house are many homes. If it weren't so, I would have told you. I am going to prepare a place for you. If I go and prepare a place for you, I will come again, and will receive you to myself; that where I am, you may be there also. You know where I go, and you know the way."

Thomas said to him, "Lord, we don't know where you are going. How can we know the way?"

Jesus said to him, ***"I am the way, the truth, and the life****. No one comes to the Father, except through me. If you had known me, you would have known my Father also. From now on, you know him, and have seen him."*

Philip said to him, "Lord, show us the Father, and that will be enough for us."

Jesus said to him, *"Have I been with you such a long time, and do you not know me, Philip? He who has seen me has seen the Father. How do you say, 'Show us the Father?' Don't you **believe** that **I am in the Father, and the Father in me**? The words that I tell you, I speak not from myself; but the Father who lives in me does his works. **Believe** me that **I am in the Father, and the Father in me**; or else **believe** me for the very works' sake. **Most certainly** I tell you, he who **believes** in me, the works that I do, he will do also; and he will do greater works than these, because <u>I am going to my Father</u>. Whatever you will ask in my name, I will do it, that the Father may be glorified in the Son. If you will ask anything in my name, I will do it. If you love me, keep my commandments. I will pray to the Father, and he will give you another Counselor, that he may be with you forever: the Spirit of truth, whom the **world** can't receive; for it doesn't see him and doesn't know him. You know him, for he lives with you, and will be in you. I will not leave you orphans. I will come to you. Yet a little while, and the **world** will see me no more; but you will see me. Because I live, you will live also. In that day you will know that **I am in my Father, and you in me, and I in you**. One who has my commandments and keeps them, that person is one who loves me. One who loves me will be loved by my Father, and I will love him, and will reveal myself to him."*

Judas (not Iscariot) said to him, "Lord, what has happened that you are about to reveal yourself to us, and not to the **world**?"

Jesus answered him, *"If a man loves me, he will keep my word. My Father will love him, and we will come to him, and make our home with him. He who doesn't love me doesn't keep my words. The word which you hear isn't mine, but the Father's who sent me. I have said these things to you while still living with you. But the Counselor, the Holy Spirit, whom the Father will send in my name, will teach you all things, and will remind you of all that I said to you. Peace I leave with you. My peace I give to you; not as the* **world** *gives, I give to you. Don't let your heart be troubled, neither let it be fearful. You heard how I told you, 'I go away, and I come to you.' If you loved me, you would have rejoiced, because I said 'I am going to my Father;' for the Father is greater than I. Now I have told you before it happens so that when it happens, you may* **believe***. I will no more speak much with you, for the prince of the* **world** *comes, and he has nothing in me. But that the* **world** *may know that I love the Father, and as the Father commanded me, even so I do. Arise, let's go from here."*

GOD AND JESUS REVELATIONS

In this chapter, Jesus says if you have seen Him, you have seen the Father; and if you know Him, you know the Father. Jesus explains He is in the Father and the Father is in

Him. Whether you believe Jesus is speaking literally or figuratively, Jesus and God are so much alike, to see one is to see the other.

Jesus also tells us to believe in God and to believe in Him. Jesus tells us He is going to heaven and will prepare a place for us. Jesus has Authority in heaven. Jesus also says He will come again, so He has ability to go to and from Heaven and Earth.

Additionally, Jesus says He will reveal Himself to those who keep His commandments. Thus, we have to direct ourselves toward keeping God's Commandments, if we want Jesus to reveal Himself to us. When we obey, we will receive Jesus's peace and His love.

IS JESUS GOD?

➢ In this chapter, what does Jesus say about God, the Father?

➢ In this chapter, what I AM declaration does Jesus make, and what else does He say about Himself?

WHAT DO YOU THINK?

➤ What kind of place do you think or dream Jesus will prepare for you in heaven?

_____
_____
_____
_____
_____
_____

➤ What one thing does Jesus tell us is "most certain" in this chapter? What beliefs and feelings do you have about this certainty?

_____
_____
_____
_____
_____
_____
_____

➤ Jesus says, if we have seen Him, then we have seen God. What does this concept tell us about who God is, and how we can see Him?

_____
_____
_____
_____
_____
_____
_____

- If you can do work that Jesus did, what kinds of works would you most love to do?

- In what ways does keeping Jesus's Commandments show your love for Him? What are you conveying to Jesus when you don't keep His Commandments?

- Jesus says He is in God, we are in Jesus, and Jesus is in US. Furthermore, Jesus says He will give us a counselor (the Holy Spirit) to be with us forever. How would you explain the indwelling of the Trinity (God, Jesus and the Holy Spirit)? How is this indwelling possible?

➢ In your understanding, what is the way, the truth, and the life?

➢ What things does Jesus give us that the world can't give us?

CHAPTER 15

"**I am the true vine**, and my Father is the farmer. Every branch in me that doesn't bear fruit, he takes away. Every branch that bears fruit, he prunes, that it may bear more fruit. You are already pruned clean because of the word which I have spoken to you. Remain in me, and I in you. As the branch can't bear fruit by itself unless it remains in the vine, so neither can you, unless you remain in me. **I am the vine**. You are the branches. He who remains in me and I in him bears much fruit, for apart from me you can do nothing. If a man doesn't remain in me, he is thrown out as a branch and is withered; and they gather them, throw them into the fire, and they are burned. If you remain in me, and my words remain in you, you will ask whatever you desire, and it will be done for you.

"In this my Father is glorified, that you bear much fruit; and so you will be my disciples. Even as the Father has loved me, I also have loved you. Remain in my love. If you keep my commandments, you will remain in my love; even as I have kept my Father's commandments, and remain in his love. I have spoken these things to you, that my joy may remain in you, and that your joy may be made full.

"This is my commandment, that you love one another, even as I have loved you. Greater love has no one than this, that someone lay down his life for his friends. You are my friends, if you do whatever I command you. No longer do I call you servants, for the servant doesn't know what his lord does. But I have called you friends, for everything that I heard from my Father, I have made known to you. You didn't choose me, but I chose you and appointed you, that you should go and bear fruit, and that your fruit should remain; that whatever you will ask of the Father in my name, he may give it to you.

"I command these things to you, that you may love one another. If the **world** hates you, you know that it has hated me before it hated you. If you were of the **world**, the **world** would love its own. But because you are not of the **world**, since I chose you out of the **world**, therefore the **world** hates you. Remember the word that I said to you: 'A servant is not greater than his lord.' If they persecuted me, they will also persecute you. If they kept my word, they will also keep yours. But they will do all these things to you for my name's sake, *because they don't know him who sent me. If I had not come and spoken to them, they would not have had sin; but now they have no excuse for their sin. He who hates me, hates my Father also. If I hadn't done among them the works which no one else did, they wouldn't have had sin. But now they have seen and also hated both me and my Father. But this happened so that the word may be fulfilled which was written in their law, 'They hated me without a cause.'*

"When the Counselor has come, whom I will send to you from the Father, the Spirit of truth, who proceeds from the Father, he will testify about me. You will also testify, because you have been with me from the beginning.

GOD AND JESUS REVELATIONS

In this chapter, Jesus says He is the Vine and God, the Father, is the farmer. Then Jesus says we are the branches that grow through Him. Since Jesus is the root of plant growth which supports us, Jesus likens Himself to us in flesh and spirit. We are flesh and spirit, like Jesus is flesh and spirit.

As our "vine," Jesus has the ability to send "the spirit of Truth to us. His ability to send the Holy Spirit shows He is of the spirit like God. Jesus is like us and He's like God.

Jesus also says, "He who hates me, hates my Father also." In this statement, Jesus links Himself as one with the Father. We can't love one and hate the other, because Jesus says they are the same. Whoever has seen Jesus has seen the Father!

IS JESUS GOD?

➢ In this chapter, what does Jesus say about God, the Father?

➤ In this chapter, what I AM declaration does Jesus make, and what other declarations does He make about Himself?

_____
_____
_____
_____
_____
_____

WHAT DO YOU THINK?

➤ Jesus says branches who don't remain in Him are gathered and thrown into the fire. As a branch on His Vine, what are some ways you can remain in Jesus throughout your lifetime?

_____
_____
_____
_____
_____
_____

➤ If Jesus is the vine and you are a branch, would you expect to be pruned as an unfruitful branch based on your current way of living? Why or why not?

_____
_____
_____
_____
_____
_____

➤ Why do you think keeping Jesus's Commandments keeps you in His love?

➤ As fully as you can, explain Jesus's commandment to love one another in this chapter. What should Christian love look like when we truly love one another?

➤ In this chapter, Jesus explains about love and hate toward Christians in the world. What kinds of things make you feel loved and hated in the world today?

➢ Jesus says, "He who hates me, hates my Father." How and where do you see this truth playing out in the world today?

___

➢ Why do people turn their backs on Jesus without seeking to know Him at all? What would you say to people to encourage them to give Jesus a chance?

___

CHAPTER 16

*"I have said these things to you so that you wouldn't be caused to stumble. They will put you out of the synagogues. Yes, the time comes that whoever kills you will think that he offers service to God. They will do these things because they have not known the Father, nor me. But I have told you these things, so that when the time comes, you may remember that I told you about them. I didn't tell you these things from the beginning, because I was with you. But now **I am going** to him who sent me, and none of you asks me, 'Where are you going?' But because I have told you these things, sorrow has filled your heart. Nevertheless I tell you the truth: It is to your advantage that I go away, for if I don't go away, the Counselor won't come to you. But if I go, I will*

*send him to you. When he has come, he will convict the **world** about sin, about righteousness, and about judgment; about sin, because they don't **believe** in me; about righteousness, because <u>I am going to my Father</u>, and you won't see me anymore; about judgment, because the prince of this **world** has been judged.*

"I still have many things to tell you, but you can't bear them now. However when he, the Spirit of truth, has come, he will guide you into all truth, for he will not speak from himself; but whatever he hears, he will speak. He will declare to you things that are coming. He will glorify me, for he will take from what is mine, and will declare it to you. All things that the Father has are mine; therefore I said that he takes of mine and will declare it to you. A little while, and you will not see me. Again a little while, and you will see me."

Some of his disciples therefore said to one another, "What is this that he says to us, *'A little while, and you won't see me, and again a little while, and you will see me;'* and, *'Because I go to the Father'?*" They said therefore, "What is this that he says, *'A little while'*? We don't know what he is saying."

Therefore Jesus perceived that they wanted to ask him, and he said to them, *"Do you inquire among yourselves concerning this, that I said, 'A little while, and you won't see me, and again a little while, and you will see me?'* **Most certainly** *I tell you that you will weep and lament, but the **world** will* *rejoice. You will be sorrowful, but your sorrow will be turned into joy. A woman, when she gives birth, has sorrow because her time has come. But when she has delivered the child, she doesn't remember the anguish any more, for the joy that a human being is born into the **world**. Therefore you now have sorrow, but I will see you again, and your heart will rejoice, and no one will take your joy away from you.*

*"In that day you will ask me no questions. **Most certainly** I tell you, whatever you may ask of the Father in my name, he will give it to you. Until now, you have asked nothing in my name. Ask, and you will receive, that your joy may be made full. I have spoken these things to you in figures of speech. But the time is coming when I will no more speak to you in figures of speech, but will tell you plainly about the Father. In that day you will ask in my name; and I don't say to you that I will pray to the Father for you, for the Father himself loves you, because you have loved me, and have **believed** that I came from God. I came from the Father, and have come into the **world**. Again, I leave the **world**, and go to the Father."*

His disciples said to him, "Behold, now you are speaking plainly, and using no figures of speech. Now we know that you know all things, and don't need for anyone to question you. By this we **believe** that you came from God."

Jesus answered them, *"Do you now **believe**? Behold, the time is coming, yes, and has now come, that you will be scattered, everyone to his own place,* *and you will leave me alone. Yet **I am not alone**, because the Father is with me. I have told you these things, that in me you may have peace. In the **world** you have trouble; but cheer up! I have overcome the **world**."*

GOD AND JESUS REVELATIONS

Jesus says everything God, the Father, has belongs to Jesus. Consider the power given to Jesus when He owns the entire kingdom. Doesn't Jesus, as the recipient of the entire Kingdom, become King of the Kingdom? If everything of God's belongs to Jesus, and Jesus rules over everything, isn't Jesus Lord and God over all of us? Is there any real difference between Jesus and God when it comes to Jesus being over everything?

People killed Jesus thinking they were offering service to God. They were judging and condemning Jesus as if they were God. Yet God didn't tell the people to judge Jesus; and Jesus spoke only of love for God and righteousness.

Think for a moment whether there is anything Jesus said which you would not expect to hear from God. Is it possible for any human to speak perfect truth for God, if God is not with or within that person?

IS JESUS GOD?

➢ In this chapter, what does Jesus say about God, the Father?

➢ What prophetic I AM declaration does Jesus make in this chapter, and what else does He say about Himself?

WHAT DO YOU THINK?

➢ Jesus said, "A time comes that whoever kills you will think he offers a service to God." Why do people who want to kill Christians think they are serving God or bettering the world?

➢ In what ways does the Holy Spirit convict you of sin, judgment, and righteousness?

➢ How does the Holy Spirit, the Spirit of Truth, affect the way you try to live your life?

➢ Jesus said His resurrection would bring unending joy for His followers. Two thousand years later, people are still joyful about Jesus's resurrection. Why? How does Jesus's resurrection influence people today?

➢ You can ask for any good or righteous thing in Jesus's name, and God, the Father, will give it to you. What would you ask for that your joy would be made full?

➢ What evidence do you see that Jesus came from God the Father?

➢ Why does your love for Jesus, and believing all He says, matter to God the Father? In what ways is your relationship with God the Father impacted by your relationship with Jesus?

➢ What troubles do you have in the world, which you are eager to overcome? In what ways might Jesus help you overcome your troubles?

CHAPTER 17

Jesus said these things, then lifting up his eyes to heaven, he said, *"Father, the time has come. Glorify your Son, that your Son may also glorify you; even as you gave him authority over all flesh, so he will give eternal life to all whom you have given him. This is eternal life, that they should know you, the only true God, and him whom you sent, Jesus Christ. I glorified you on the earth. I have accomplished the work which you have given me to do. Now, Father, glorify me with your own self with the glory which I had with you before the **world** existed. I revealed your name to the people whom you have given me out of the **world**. They were yours, and you have given them to me. They have kept your word. Now they have known that all things whatever you have given me* *are from you, for the words which you have given me I have given to them, and they received them, and knew for sure that I came from you. They have **believed** that you sent me. I pray for them. I don't pray for the **world**, but for those whom you have given me, for they are yours. All things that are mine are yours, and yours are mine, and I am glorified in them. I am no more in the **world**, but these are in the **world**, and I am coming to you. Holy Father, keep them through your name which you have given me, that they may be one, even as we are.*

*While I was with them in the **world**, I kept them in your name. I have kept those whom you have given me. None of them is lost except the son of destruction, that the Scripture might be fulfilled. But now I come to you, and I say these things in the **world**, that they may have my joy made full in themselves. I have given them your word. The **world** hated them, because they are not of the **world**, even as **I am not of the world**. I pray not that you would take them from the **world**, but that you would keep them from the evil one. They are not of the **world** even as **I am not of the world**. Sanctify them in your truth.*

*Your word is truth. As you sent me into the **world**, even so I have sent them into the **world**. For their sakes I sanctify myself, that they themselves also may be sanctified in truth. Not for these only do I pray, but for those also who will **believe** in me through their word, that they may all be one; even as you, Father, are in me, and I in you, that* *they also may be one in us; that the **world** may **believe** that you sent me. The glory which you have given me, I have given to them; that they may be one, even as we are one; I in them, and you in me, that they may be perfected into one; that the **world** may know that you sent me and loved them, even as you loved me. Father, I desire that they also whom you have given me be with me where I am, that they may see my glory, which you have given me, for you loved me before the foundation of the **world**. Righteous Father, the **world** hasn't known you, but I knew you; and these knew that you sent me. I made known to them your name, and will make it known; that the love with which you loved me may be in them, and I in them."*

GOD AND JESUS REVELATIONS

Jesus speaks to God about glorifying both of them through the events which are about to happen. He also speaks of revealing God to the world. Jesus reiterates all that is in the world belongs to Himself, because God gave it to Him. Jesus prays everyone in the world will be one, as Jesus and God are one.

Lastly, Jesus talks about being with God before the foundation of the world. If you recall, this book's first chapter says "all things were made through Him," so Jesus is the creator of the world. Again, with the rules of logic, if Jesus is the creator of the world, then it's logical He is also God of the world.

IS JESUS GOD?

➢ In this chapter, what does Jesus say about the relationship between Jesus and God, the Father?

➢ In this chapter, what declaration(s) does Jesus make about Himself?

WHAT DO YOU THINK?

➢ What differences does Jesus point out between those who belong to God versus those who belong to this world? Do you belong to God? Whether you belong to God or not, why are these differences critical for you to understand?

➢ How does God the Father give people to Jesus? Do you believe you've been given to Jesus? Why or why not?

➢ What makes it easy or difficult for you to believe God sent Jesus to the world, and sent Jesus to you?

➢ What do you think Jesus means when He says, this is eternal life, that they should know you, the only true God? In what ways is knowing God the foundation for eternal life?

➢ In the second half of this chapter, Jesus prays that we may be one, even as He and God are one. Explain how God and Jesus are one? How we can similarly be one with each other and with Jesus and God.

- How is our joy made full through the things Jesus teaches us? Do you feel like you have more joy because you know Jesus? Why or why not?

- How does perfect unity among Christians (being one with each other, God, and Jesus) help people in the world believe God sent Jesus? How does unity help people believe Jesus is the way, the truth, and the life?

- When you get to know Jesus and accept God's truth and love, how are you made holy? How does God fill you with His love?

CHAPTER 18

When Jesus had spoken these words, he went out with his disciples over the brook Kidron, where there was a garden, into which he and his disciples entered. Now Judas, who betrayed him, also knew the place, for Jesus often met there with his disciples. Judas then, having taken a detachment of soldiers and officers from the chief priests and the Pharisees, came there with lanterns, torches, and weapons. Jesus therefore, knowing all the things that were happening to him, went out, and said to them, "Who are you looking for?"

They answered him, "Jesus of Nazareth."

Jesus said to them, *"I am he."*

Judas also, who betrayed him, was standing with them.

When therefore he said to them, *"I am he,"* they went backward, and fell to the ground.

Again therefore he asked them, *"Who are you looking for?"*

They said, "Jesus of Nazareth."

Jesus answered, *"I told you that I am he. If therefore you seek me, let these go their way,"* that the word might be fulfilled which he spoke, "Of those whom you have given me, I have lost none."

Simon Peter therefore, having a sword, drew it, struck the high priest's servant, and cut off his right ear. The servant's name was Malchus.

Jesus therefore said to Peter, *"Put the sword into its sheath. The cup which the Father has given me, shall I not surely drink it?"*

So the detachment, the commanding officer, and the officers of the Jews seized Jesus and bound him, and led him to Annas first, for he was father-in-law to Caiaphas, who was high priest that year. Now it was Caiaphas who advised the Jews that it was expedient that one man should perish for the people. Simon Peter followed Jesus, as did another disciple. Now that disciple was known to the high priest, and entered in with Jesus into the court of the high priest; but Peter was standing at the door outside. So the other disciple, who was known to the high priest, went out and spoke to her who kept the door, and brought in Peter. Then the maid who kept the door said to Peter, "Are you also one of this man's disciples?"

He said, "I am not."

Now the servants and the officers were standing there, having made a fire of coals, for it was cold. They were warming themselves. Peter was with them, standing and warming himself. The high priest therefore asked Jesus about his disciples and about his teaching. Jesus answered him, *"I spoke openly to the **world**. I always taught in synagogues, and in the temple, where the Jews always meet. I said nothing in secret. Why do you ask me? Ask those who have heard me what I said to them. Behold, they know the things which I said."*

When he had said this, one of the officers standing by slapped Jesus with his hand, saying, "Do you answer the high priest like that?"

Jesus answered him, *"If I have spoken evil, testify of the evil; but if well, why do you beat me?"*

Annas sent him bound to Caiaphas, the high priest. Now Simon Peter was standing and warming himself. They said therefore to him, "You aren't also one of his disciples, are you?"

He denied it and said, "I am not."

One of the servants of the high priest, being a relative of him whose ear Peter had cut off, said, "Didn't I see you in the garden with him?"

Peter therefore denied it again, and immediately the rooster crowed.

They led Jesus therefore from Caiaphas into the Praetorium. It was early, and they themselves didn't enter into the

Praetorium, that they might not be defiled, but might eat the Passover. Pilate therefore went out to them, and said, "What accusation do you bring against this man?"

They answered him, "If this man weren't an evildoer, we wouldn't have delivered him up to you."

Pilate therefore said to them, "Take him yourselves, and judge him according to your law."

Therefore the Jews said to him, "It is illegal for us to put anyone to death," that the word of Jesus might be fulfilled, which he spoke, signifying by what kind of death he should die.

Pilate therefore entered again into the Praetorium, called Jesus, and said to him, "Are you the King of the Jews?"

Jesus answered him, *"Do you say this by yourself, or did others tell you about me?"*

Pilate answered, "I'm not a Jew, am I? Your own nation and the chief priests delivered you to me. What have you done?"

Jesus answered, *"My Kingdom is not of this **world**. If my Kingdom were of this **world**, then my servants would fight, that I wouldn't be delivered to the Jews. But now my Kingdom is not from here."*

Pilate therefore said to him, "Are you a king then?"

*Jesus answered, "You say that I am a king. For this reason I have been born, and for this reason I have come into the **world**, that I should testify to the truth. Everyone who is of the truth listens to my voice."*

Pilate said to him, "What is truth?"

When he had said this, he went out again to the Jews, and said to them, "I find no basis for a charge against him. But you have a custom, that I should release someone to you at the Passover. Therefore, do you want me to release to you the King of the Jews?"

Then they all shouted again, saying, "Not this man, but Barabbas!" Now Barabbas was a robber.

GOD AND JESUS REVELATIONS

When the soldiers took Jesus away, the people probably doubted Jesus was the Messiah. People would assume the true Messiah would fight back. Since Jesus didn't fight back at all, they didn't think Jesus was God.

Perhaps Jesus's manner of death leads you to question Jesus's divinity too. It's a question each of us has to wrestle with. Most of us ask ourselves, "Why didn't Jesus fight back or pick another way to save the world?"

Jesus's kingdom is not in this world. After His death He returned to His kingdom where He has full reign and righteousness is a way of life.

Here on Earth, Satan is constantly battling to win people over to himself. Thus, it can sometimes seem like Jesus and God are not Lord over everything on Earth. Yet, even in His death and letting wickedness kill Him, Jesus was carrying out God's plan to reveal His glory.

Jesus couldn't prove His power over life and death without dying and resurrecting. Although it is difficult for us to reason through the spiritual nature of Jesus, we know Jesus willingly went to His death. It takes a divine nature to walk straight into your certain death without fighting back.

Even though Jesus submitted to the authorities, they only had authority over Jesus because He yielded authority to them. The Pharisees thought they put Jesus in His place. But, the Pharisees were blind to Jesus's divinity and to what would happen after they killed Jesus!

IS JESUS GOD?

➢ In this chapter, what does Jesus say about Himself, His Kingdom, and Himself as a King?

➢ In this chapter, what I AM declaration does Jesus make about Himself?

WHAT DO YOU THINK?

➢ Why did Peter lie about knowing Jesus when Peter swore he'd never leave Jesus? Do you think you might deny Jesus under similar circumstances? Why or why not?

➢ Why do people get angry with others, as they did with Jesus, even when a person is speaking the truth?

➢ What is it about Jesus which might make people fall to the ground when they encounter Him?

➢ The Jews were evasive about telling Pilate what Jesus did to deserve death. Why do you think they were evasive with their answer? What was really driving their desire to have Jesus crucified?

➢ How do you think the world would be different if Jesus had saved Himself from crucifixion?

- If Jesus's kingdom is not of this world, where do you believe Jesus's Kingdom is located? What makes you believe that?

- Jesus says, "Everyone who is of the truth listens to My voice." How can we know if we are of the truth and can hear Jesus's voice?

- Jesus said He came into the world to testify to God's truth. What is God's truth, as you understand it?

CHAPTER 19

So Pilate then took Jesus, and flogged him. The soldiers twisted thorns into a crown, and put it on his head, and dressed him in a purple garment. They kept saying, "Hail, King of the Jews!" and they kept slapping him.

Then Pilate went out again, and said to them, "Behold, I bring him out to you, that you may know that I find no basis for a charge against him."

Jesus therefore came out, wearing the crown of thorns and the purple garment. Pilate said to them, "Behold, the man!"

When therefore the chief priests and the officers saw him, they shouted, saying, "Crucify! Crucify!"

Pilate said to them, "Take him yourselves, and crucify him, for I find no basis for a charge against him."

The Jews answered him, "We have a law, and by our law he ought to die, because he made himself the Son of God."

When therefore Pilate heard this saying, he was more afraid. He entered into the Praetorium again, and said to Jesus, "Where are you from?" But Jesus gave him no answer. Pilate therefore said to him, "Aren't you speaking to me? Don't you know that I have power to release you and have power to crucify you?"

Jesus answered, *"You would have no power at all against me, unless it were given to you from above. Therefore he who delivered me to you has greater sin."*

At this, Pilate was seeking to release him, but the Jews cried out, saying, "If you release this man, you aren't Caesar's friend! Everyone who makes himself a king speaks against Caesar!"

When Pilate therefore heard these words, he brought Jesus out and sat down on the judgment seat at a place called "The Pavement", but in Hebrew, "Gabbatha."

Now it was the Preparation Day of the Passover, at about the sixth hour. He said to the Jews, "Behold, your King!" They cried out, "Away with him! Away with him! Crucify him!"

Pilate said to them, "Shall I crucify your King?"

The chief priests answered, "We have no king but Caesar!"

So then he delivered him to them to be crucified. So they took Jesus and led him away. He went out, bearing his cross, to the place called "The Place of a Skull", which is called in Hebrew, "Golgotha", where they crucified him, and with him two others, on either side one, and Jesus in the middle. Pilate wrote a title also, and put it on the cross. There was written, "JESUS OF NAZARETH, THE KING OF THE JEWS." Therefore many of the Jews read this title, for the place where Jesus was crucified was near the city; and it was written in Hebrew, in Latin, and in Greek. The chief priests of the Jews therefore said to Pilate, "Don't write, 'The King of the Jews,' but, 'he said, "I am King of the Jews." ' "

Pilate answered, "What I have written, I have written."

Then the soldiers, when they had crucified Jesus, took his garments and made four parts, to every soldier a part; and also the coat. Now the coat was without seam, woven from the top throughout. Then they said to one another, "Let's not tear it, but cast lots for it to decide whose it will be," that the Scripture might be fulfilled, which says,

"They parted my garments among them. For my cloak they cast lots."

Therefore the soldiers did these things. But standing by Jesus' cross were his mother, his mother's sister, Mary the wife of Clopas, and Mary Magdalene. Therefore when Jesus saw his mother, and the disciple whom he loved standing there, he said to his mother, *"Woman, behold, your son!"* Then he said to the disciple,

"Behold, your mother!" From that hour, the disciple took her to his own home.

After this, Jesus, seeing that all things were now finished, that the Scripture might be fulfilled, said, *"I am thirsty."* Now a vessel full of vinegar was set there; so they put a sponge full of the vinegar on hyssop, and held it at his mouth. When Jesus therefore had received the vinegar, he said, *"It is finished."* He bowed his head, and gave up his spirit.

Therefore the Jews, because it was the Preparation Day, so that the bodies wouldn't remain on the cross on the Sabbath (for that Sabbath was a special one), asked of Pilate that their legs might be broken, and that they might be taken away. Therefore the soldiers came, and broke the legs of the first, and of the other who was crucified with him; but when they came to Jesus, and saw that he was already dead, they didn't break his legs. However one of the soldiers pierced his side with a spear, and immediately blood and water came out. He who has seen has testified, and his testimony is true. He knows that he tells the truth, that you may **believe**. For these things happened that the Scripture might be fulfilled, "A bone of him will not be broken." Again another Scripture says, "They will look on him whom they pierced."

After these things, Joseph of Arimathaea, being a disciple of Jesus, but secretly for fear of the Jews, asked of Pilate that he might take away Jesus' body. Pilate gave him permission. He came therefore and took away his body.

Nicodemus, who at first came to Jesus by night, also came bringing a mixture of myrrh and aloes, about a hundred Roman pounds. So they took Jesus' body, and bound it in linen cloths with the spices, as the custom of the Jews is to bury. Now in the place where he was crucified there was a garden. In the garden was a new tomb in which no man had ever yet been laid. Then because of the Jews' Preparation Day (for the tomb was near at hand) they laid Jesus there.

GOD AND JESUS REVELATIONS

It takes restraint and godliness to submit to mocking, beating, and name-calling. Jesus submitted without any words or actions of self-defense. Jesus let His oppressors do to Him whatever they wished. Yet, Jesus's killers only had the authority God and Jesus gave to them, and they gave the killers authority over Jesus's life.

The Jewish leaders wanted Jesus killed because they said, "He made himself the Son of God." Do you think they considered, even for a moment, it was God who made Jesus the son of God?

The Jews also objected to the crucifixion sign saying, "Jesus of Nazareth, The King of the Jews." They didn't accept or believe Jesus was their King. Yet Jesus was their King, and they were blind to the truth.

Lastly, in this chapter it says Jesus bowed his head, and gave up His spirit. That wording indicates Jesus willfully died on the cross. Since Jesus knew He would rise after His death, He knew dying wasn't the end of His life.

Once He died, Jesus no longer had to live with defiant, hateful people on earth. The hardest part of His self-sacrifice was over. Jesus's resurrected eternal life was about" to begin a whole new era!

IS JESUS GOD?

➤ In this chapter, the only thing Jesus says related to God is, "You would have no power at all against me, unless it were given to you from above." When it comes to Jesus being the Messiah, why is the origin of His power important for us to understand?

➤ In this chapter, Jesus makes NO declarations about Himself. Why do you think Jesus stayed silent, and did not say anything to defend Himself when questioned?

WHAT DO YOU THINK?

➤ Why do you think the soldiers slapped, taunted, and mocked Jesus? How you think a crowd of haters would behave toward Jesus today?

➤ For what reason(s) would a leader like Pilate allow the crucifixion of an innocent man? Under what circumstances might something similar happen in today's world?

- If the Jews killed Jesus because "He made himself the Son of God," what do you think the Jews would do today if someone came today saying he was the son of God?

- Do you think it would have mattered if Jesus tried to defend Himself against the charge of "making Himself the Son of God?" Why or why not?

- Why is crucifying Jesus under the sign "The King of the Jews," versus, "He said, 'I Am King of the Jews,'" a crucial difference? What are the ramifications of each sign?

➢ Describe as fully as you can, what was "finished" when Jesus died on the cross?

➢ There are many details shared in this chapter regarding ancient prophetic scriptures being fulfilled in the events of Jesus's life and crucifixion. Why is it important for us to take note of the ancient prophecies fulfilled by Jesus?

➢ Who is currently king of your life? Who do you want to be king of your life and why?

CHAPTER 20

Now on the first day of the week, Mary Magdalene went early, while it was still dark, to the tomb, and saw the stone taken away from the tomb. Therefore she ran and came to Simon Peter and to the other disciple whom Jesus loved, and said to them, "They have taken away the Lord out of the tomb, and we don't know where they have laid him!"

Therefore Peter and the other disciple went out, and they went toward the tomb. They both ran together. The other disciple outran Peter, and came to the tomb first. Stooping and looking in, he saw the linen cloths lying, yet he didn't enter in. Then Simon Peter came, following him, and entered into the tomb. He saw the linen cloths lying, and the cloth that had been on his head, not lying with the linen cloths, but rolled up in a place by itself. So then the other disciple who came first to the tomb also entered in, and he saw and **believed**. For as yet they didn't know the Scripture, that he must rise from the dead. So the disciples went away again to their own homes.

But Mary was standing outside at the tomb weeping. So as she wept, she stooped and looked into the tomb, and she saw two angels in white sitting, one at the head, and one at the feet, where the body of Jesus had lain. They asked her, "Woman, why are you weeping?"

She said to them, "Because they have taken away my Lord, and I don't know where they have laid him." When she had said this, she turned around and saw Jesus standing, and didn't know that it was Jesus.

Jesus said to her, *"Woman, why are you weeping? Who are you looking for?"*

She, supposing him to be the gardener, said to him, "Sir, if you have carried him away, tell me where you have laid him, and I will take him away."

Jesus said to her, *"Mary."*

She turned and said to him, "Rabboni!" which is to say, "Teacher!"

Jesus said to her, *"Don't hold me, for I haven't yet ascended to my Father; but go to my brothers and tell them, '***I am ascending to my Father and your Father, to my God and your God.***' "*

Mary Magdalene came and told the

disciples that she had seen the Lord, and that he had said these things to her. When therefore it was evening on that day, the first day of the week, and when the doors were locked where the disciples were assembled, for fear of the Jews, Jesus came and stood in the middle, and said to them, *"Peace be to you."*

When he had said this, he showed them his hands and his side. The disciples therefore were glad when they saw the Lord. Jesus therefore said to them again, *"Peace be to you. As the Father has sent me, even so I send you."*

When he had said this, he breathed on them, and said to them, *"Receive the Holy Spirit! If you forgive anyone's sins, they have been forgiven them. If you retain anyone's sins, they have been retained."*

But Thomas, one of the twelve, called Didymus, wasn't with them when Jesus came. The other disciples therefore said to him, "We have seen the Lord!"

But he said to them, "Unless I see in his hands the print of the nails, put my finger into the print of the nails, and put my hand into his side, I will not **believe**."

After eight days again his disciples were inside and Thomas was with them. Jesus came, the doors being locked, and stood in the middle, and said, *"Peace be to you."* Then he said to Thomas, *"Reach here your finger, and see my hands. Reach here your hand, and put it into my side. Don't be un**believing**, but **believing**."*

Thomas answered him, "My Lord and my God!"

Jesus said to him, *"Because you have seen me, you have **believed**. Blessed are those who have not seen, and have **believed**."*

Therefore Jesus did many other signs in the presence of his disciples, which are not written in this book; but these are written, that you may **believe** that Jesus is the Christ, the Son of God, and that **believing** you may have life in his name.

GOD AND JESUS REVELATIONS

This is the chapter of Jesus's eternal triumph and victory. Jesus says, "I am ascending to My Father and your Father, to my God and your God." Thus, in this chapter, Jesus speaks of Himself as distinctly separate from God the Father.

Jesus then breathed the Holy Spirit into His disciples. Jesus, like God, can impart the Holy Spirit into anyone whom He chooses. Jesus asks us to believe. All the more blessed are we who have not actually seen Jesus, yet believe Jesus is the Son of God.

IS JESUS GOD?

➢ What does Jesus say about being sent by God, the Father? Why is this important?

➢ What declaration(s) does Jesus make about Himself in this chapter?

WHAT DO YOU THINK?

➢ See yourself going to Jesus's tomb. You see His burial cloth rolled up and set aside, but Jesus is nowhere to be seen. What questions and thoughts come to your mind?

___

➢ Why do you think those closest to Jesus didn't recognize Him? Why did some of His disciples doubt Jesus was alive?

___

➢ When you receive(d) the Holy Spirit from Jesus, what expectations do you think Jesus has for your understanding, following, and serving Him?

___

➤ Jesus says He sends us, as His Father sent Him. In your life, what do you think Jesus expects sending you to look like?

_____
_____
_____
_____
_____

➤ Since you have the power to forgive or retain others' sins, what do you think Jesus expects you to do with your power to forgive others?

_____
_____
_____
_____
_____

➤ Jesus tells us, "Don't be unbelieving, but believing." What strengthens your beliefs? How can you strengthen your belief in Jesus?

_____
_____
_____
_____
_____

➤ At this point in our reading, do you believe Jesus Is God? Why or why not?

_____
_____
_____
_____
_____

CHAPTER 21

After these things, Jesus revealed himself again to the disciples at the sea of Tiberias. He revealed himself this way. Simon Peter, Thomas called Didymus, Nathanael of Cana in Galilee, and the sons of Zebedee, and two others of his disciples were together. Simon Peter said to them, "I'm going fishing."

They told him, "We are also coming with you." They immediately went out, and entered into the boat. That night, they caught nothing. But when day had already come, Jesus stood on the beach, yet the disciples didn't know that it was Jesus. Jesus therefore said to them, *"Children, have you anything to eat?"*

They answered him, "No."

He said to them, *"Cast the net on the*

right side of the boat, and you will find some."

They cast it therefore, and now they weren't able to draw it in for the multitude of fish. That disciple therefore whom Jesus loved said to Peter, "It's the Lord!"

So when Simon Peter heard that it was the Lord, he wrapped his coat around himself (for he was naked), and threw himself into the sea. But the other disciples came in the little boat (for they were not far from the land, but about two hundred cubits away), dragging the net full of fish. So when they got out on the land, they saw a fire of coals there, with fish and bread laid on it.

Jesus said to them, *"Bring some of the fish which you have just caught."*

Simon Peter went up, and drew the net to land, full of one hundred fifty-three great fish. Even though there were so many, the net wasn't torn.

Jesus said to them, *"Come and eat breakfast!"*

None of the disciples dared inquire of him, "Who are you?" knowing that it was the Lord.

Then Jesus came and took the bread, gave it to them, and the fish likewise. This is now the third time that Jesus was revealed to his disciples after he had risen from the dead. So when they had eaten their breakfast, Jesus said to Simon Peter, *"Simon, son of Jonah, do you love me more than these?"*

He said to him, "Yes, Lord; you know that I have affection for you."

He said to him, *"Feed my lambs."* He said to him again a second time, *"Simon, son of Jonah, do you love me?"*

He said to him, "Yes, Lord; you know that I have affection for you."

He said to him, *"Tend my sheep."* He said to him the third time, *"Simon, son of Jonah, do you have affection for me?"*

Peter was grieved because he asked him the third time, *"Do you have affection for me?"* He said to him, "Lord, you know everything. You know that I have affection for you."

Jesus said to him, *"Feed my sheep.* **Most certainly** *I tell you, when you were young, you dressed yourself and walked where you wanted to. But when you are old, you will stretch out your hands, and another will dress you and carry you where you don't want to go."*

Now he said this, signifying by what kind of death he would glorify God. When he had said this, he said to him, *"Follow me."*

Then Peter, turning around, saw a disciple following.

This was the disciple whom Jesus loved, the one who had also leaned on Jesus' breast at the supper and asked, "Lord, who is going to betray you?" Peter seeing him, said to Jesus, "Lord, what about this man?"

Jesus said to him, *"If I desire that he stay until I come, what is that to you? You follow me."* This saying therefore went out among the brothers, that this disciple wouldn't die. Yet Jesus didn't say to him that he wouldn't die, but, *"If I desire that he stay until I come, what is that to you?"*

This is the disciple who testifies about these things, and wrote these things. We know that his witness is true. There are also many other things which Jesus did, which if they would all be written, I suppose that even the **world** itself wouldn't have room for the books that would be written.

GOD AND JESUS REVELATIONS

Jesus appears to many people, alive and resurrected after his death. His appearances led to the historical recording of Jesus's life, death, and resurrection by the writers of the Gospels. This book is one of the great historical accounts written shortly after Jesus's resurrection and ascension back to heaven.

During the time Jesus was resurrected on earth, Jesus prophesied Peter's future. Jesus also performed the miracle of the great fish catch. After His resurrection, we see Jesus perform more miracles and prophesy the future. Jesus doesn't say anything else about God, but He does prove He still has the sovereign characteristics of God.

IS JESUS GOD?

➢ What do Jesus's commands to feed and tend His sheep imply about His lordship? How would you interpret these commands, if they were spoken to you by Jesus?

WHAT DO YOU THINK?

➢ After His resurrection, Jesus performed the miracle of the great fish catch for the disciples. Why are additional miracles from Jesus helpful for building our faith, even though many of us already believe Jesus is who He says He is?

➢ In this chapter, what instructions does Jesus give His disciples, which might also apply to you and all Christians?

➢ Metaphorically speaking, in what kinds of thoughts and actions would you feel like you were standing naked before Jesus?

➤ When Peter asked Jesus, "What about John?" Jesus basically tells Peter it's none of his business. Jesus tells Peter to tend to himself in following Jesus. Why do we need to tend to ourselves before worrying about others, especially when following Jesus?

➤ Matthew Henry's concise commentary says three times Jesus asked Peter if he loves Him, because Peter denied Christ Jesus three times. Jesus was testing Peter's commitment to Jesus. When Jesus tests your faith, do you think you'll become more adamant about your faith, or would you think Jesus has no faith in you? Why?

➤ Peter denied Jesus at Jesus's trial. Jesus asked Peter whether he loves Jesus more than the other disciples. How would you rank and compare your love for Jesus when compared to the disciples?

➢ Jesus tells Peter, "Feed my lambs, tend my sheep, and feed my sheep." We are called to help others who follow Jesus. How can you help tend to and feed Jesus's flock?

➢ Jesus is very clear and precise about His directive to "Follow Me." Since Jesus was physically leaving the world, and has been physically away from the world ever since, exactly how can you follow Jesus? What can you do to follow Jesus faithfully?

BONUS CHAPTERS: HEBREWS 1 & 2

Chapter 1

God, having in the past spoken to the fathers through the prophets at many times and in various ways, has at the end of these days spoken to us *by his Son, whom he appointed heir of all things, through whom also he made the **worlds**.*

His Son is the radiance of his glory, the very image of his substance, and upholding all things by the word of his power, who, when he had by himself purified us of our sins, sat down on the right hand of the Majesty on high, having become as much better than the angels as the more excellent name he has inherited is better than theirs. For to which of the angels did he say at any time,

"You are my Son. Today I have become your father?" and again, "I will be to him a Father, and he will be to me a Son?

When he again brings in the firstborn into the **world** he says, "Let all the angels of God worship him."

Of the angels he says, "He makes his angels winds, and his servants a flame of fire."

But of the Son he says, "Your throne, O God, is forever and ever. The scepter of uprightness is the scepter of your Kingdom. You have loved righteousness and hated iniquity; therefore God, your God, has anointed you with the oil of gladness above your fellows."

And, "You, Lord, in the beginning, laid the foundation of the earth. The heavens are the works of your hands. They will perish, but you continue. They all will grow old like a garment does. You will roll them up like a mantle, and they will be changed; but you are the same. Your years won't fail."

But which of the angels has he told at any time, "Sit at my right hand, until I make your enemies the footstool of your feet?"

Aren't they all serving spirits, sent out to do service for the sake of those who will inherit salvation?

Chapter 2

Therefore we ought to pay greater attention to the things that were heard, lest perhaps we drift away. For if the word spoken through angels proved steadfast, and every transgression and disobedience received a just penalty, how will we escape if we neglect so great a salvation—which at the first having been spoken through the Lord, was confirmed to us by those who heard, God also testifying with them, both by signs and wonders, by various works of power and by gifts of the Holy Spirit, according to his own will?

For he didn't subject the **world** to come, of which we speak, to angels. But one has somewhere testified, saying,

"What is man, that you think of him?
Or the son of man, that you care for him?
You made him a little lower than the angels. You crowned him with glory and honor. You have put all things in subjection under his feet."

For in that he subjected all things to him, he left nothing that is not subject to him. But now we don't see all things subjected to him, yet. But we see him who has been made a little lower than the angels, Jesus, because of the suffering of death crowned with glory and honor, that by the grace of God he should taste of death for everyone.

For it became him, for whom are all things, and through whom are all things, in bringing many children to glory, to make the author of their salvation perfect through sufferings. For both he who sanctifies and those who are sanctified are all from one, for which cause he is not ashamed to call them brothers, saying,

"I will declare your name to my brothers. Among the congregation I will sing your praise."

Again, "I will put my trust in him."

Again, "Behold, here I am with the children whom God has given me." Since then the children have shared in flesh and blood, he also himself in the same way partook of the same, that through death he might bring to nothing him who had the power of death, that is, the devil, and might deliver all of them who through fear of death were all their lifetime subject to bondage. For **most certainly**, he doesn't give help to angels, but he gives help to the offspring of Abraham.

Therefore he was obligated in all things to be made like his brothers, that he might become a merciful and faithful high priest in things pertaining to God, to make atonement for the sins of the people. For in that he himself has suffered being tempted, he is able to help those who are tempted.

GOD AND JESUS REVELATIONS

In these chapters from the Book of Hebrews, we again read the world was made through Jesus. We again read Jesus laid the foundation of the earth. We also read that Jesus is the very image of God.

Yet, this scripture says Jesus was made like his brothers, into a man. Jesus had to become a man, so He may become merciful and faithful high priest in the things pertaining to God. Jesus also had to make atonement for the sins of people. So Jesus delivers us from death, and He is our Lord and Redeemer.

God says of His Son, Jesus, "Your throne, O God, is forever and ever." It's kind of peculiar for God to call His Son "God," yet His Son Jesus is God over all the Earth. If Jesus and God are one and the same, is Jesus talking to Himself? Or is Jesus's deity over all the earth simply being acknowledged by God, the Father?

Whether Jesus and God the Father are a single spiritual entity or not, we know that Jesus is God over all of the earth. Therefore, Jesus IS God, our God, over all of the Earth. Jesus is also in one accord with God the Father. In conclusion, Jesus is our God and heavenly Father, whether He and God, the Father, are exactly the same person or not.

IS JESUS GOD?

> In these two chapters, what does Apostle Paul say about God, the Father?

> In these two chapters, what declarations does Apostle Paul make about Jesus?

WHAT DO YOU THINK?

> God spoke through Jesus, and Jesus upheld all things by the power of His Word. What kinds of things do we learn about God from Jesus's words?

➢ Since God appointed Jesus heir of all things, all things are under the control of Jesus. If Jesus inherited all things and controls all things, is there anything God controls? Explain how you understand the status of God's power and control on earth?

___

➢ Since Jesus is the very image of the substance of God, how are Jesus and God similar? In what ways are they different?

___

➢ God said to Jesus, "You are my Son. Today I have become your Father. And again, I will be to Him a Father, and He will be to Me a Son." How do these statements show Jesus and God are two distinct people, as far as how humans understand relationships?

___

- Of the Son, God says these two things:
    1. "Your throne, O God, is forever and ever;"
    2. "You, Lord, in the beginning, laid the foundation of the Earth."

    How do these two statements show Jesus is God by God's own words about Jesus?

- To what group of people would you want to be sent, for the sake of those who will inherit salvation?

- Who do you think you are to God, that God would think of you and care for you with his steadfast love?

➤ We are told to pay great attention to what we heard in the Word, so as not to drift away and receive "just penalty" for our sins. What are just penalties for our sins? What are some things you can do to ensure you do not drift away?

_____
_____
_____
_____
_____
_____
_____
_____
_____
_____
_____

Go and do the things which will prevent you from drifting away from Jesus!

WHAT'S NEXT?

Congratulations on completing the Gospel Book of John, and this Is Jesus God? exploration. Now that you've met Jesus and studied about who He is, you might wonder, "What's next?"

Have you prayed a prayer asking Jesus to be the Lord of your life, and asked Him to help you overcome your sins? If so, then your next step is getting baptized and getting to know Jesus more deeply. Too many people rely on what others say, and they don't ever get to know Jesus for themselves.

Romans 16:18 warns us about people who lead others astray. Romans says, "For those who are such don't serve our Lord, Jesus Christ, but their own belly; and by their smooth and flattering speech, they deceive the hearts of the innocent." If you don't get to know Jesus for yourself, then people will be able to deceive you.

Additionally, Jesus can't be as effective in your life if you don't develop a relationship with Him. Everything Jesus taught is important for your spiritual growth. Thus, it's critical for you to study everything taught in the Bible.

In Matthew 11:29-30, Jesus says, "Take my yoke upon you, and learn from me, for I am gentle and lowly in heart, and you will find rest for your souls. For my yoke is easy, and my burden is light." Studying Jesus helps build your faith in Him. Having faith in Him makes your life less burdensome. It's easier to navigate the really difficult phases in life when you have Jesus in your life. Knowing Jesus helps you understand the eternal outlook of your life.

Do you remember what Jesus taught about how your faith affects the outcome of your prayers? If you remember, then you know it's important for you to have faith in Jesus, so you'll have effective prayers. The best way to strengthen your faith is to get to know Jesus on a personal level.

You can get to know Jesus pretty well by reading all four of the Gospel books in the New Testament. They are the books titled Matthew, Mark, Luke, and John in the Christian Bible. Each Gospel will give you different insights into who Jesus is and what He taught.

The four Gospels cover Jesus' actions and teachings in detail. Mark gives an account of Jesus' life through the eyes of Jesus' companions—His disciples. Mark was the scribe for Apostle Peter's eye-witness account. Plus, Mark knew several of the disciples.

My recommendation is to dive into a study of the Gospel of Mark, with my Journal Bible Study titled, "Who Is Jesus?" for your next study. It is the first book published in this Psalm 30 Publishing Journal Bible Study series. It's also the first Gospel book written in the Bible.

Luke was a physician and a traveling companion of the Apostle Paul. Luke investigated Jesus to give a detailed account of Jesus' life.

Matthew and John give their firsthand, eyewitness testimonies about Jesus too. They were among the 12 chosen apostles of Jesus.

If you've already read the Gospel of Mark, you can find the other journal Bible studies listed on my website. You'll find the website at: JournalBibleStudy.com.

Going forward, how will you get to know Jesus better? What are Jesus's expectations for you? What are your expectations for your own relationship with Jesus?

You can study the New Testament, Old Testament, or read your whole Bible. Whichever you read, you will grow closer to God for as long as you study your Bible! God's Word is living and active. It will bring you new insights and spiritual growth throughout your lifetime.

When you study Jesus's teachings and God's expectations, prepare to be amazed. May God bless you throughout your journey. May the Lord give you great insights and inspiration. I pray He develops you into a strong, spirited follower of Jesus Christ!

DO YOU WANT TO JESUS TO BECOME YOUR LORD?

If you haven't asked Jesus to come into your life as your Savior yet, it's easy to do. All you have to do is ask Jesus to be your Lord and Savior. Here's what the Bible says about being saved:

- **Romans 10:9-10** says, "If you will confess with your mouth that Jesus is Lord, and **believe** in your heart that God raised him from the dead, you will be saved. For with the heart, one **believes** unto righteousness; and with the mouth confession is made unto salvation."

- **Romans 10:13** says, "Whoever will call on the name of the Lord will be saved." The name of the Lord is Jesus.

- **Mark 16:16** says, "He who **believes** and is baptized will be saved; but he who dis**believes** will be condemned." Here, belief is the main key to being saved, but baptism is an act of faith for those who **believe**.

Jesus will come into your life and save you. It's as easy as believing Jesus is God's Son. With all sincerity, ask Jesus to save you and to become Lord in your life. You can ask Jesus by praying the following prayer:

"Lord Jesus, I believe you are God's Son, and God resurrected you from the dead. Please come into my life as my Lord and Savior, and save me from my sins. In Jesus' name I pray, Amen."

For a deeper understanding of the concept of being saved, let's look at the book of John. Chapter 3:14-21 (quoted below) should help you. Keep in mind, when these verses refer to 'light,' they mean Jesus, because He is the Light to the world:

"As Moses lifted up the serpent in the wilderness, even so must the Son of Man (Jesus) be lifted up, that whoever believes in Him should not perish, but have eternal life. *For God so loved the world, that He gave His one and only Son (Jesus), that whoever believes in Him should not perish, but have eternal life.* For God didn't send His Son into the world to judge the world, but that the world should be saved through Him (Jesus). The person who believes in Him (Jesus) is not judged. The person who doesn't believe has been judged already, because he has not believed in the name of the one and only Son of God. This is the judgment, that the light (Jesus) has come into the world, and men loved the darkness rather than the light; for their works were evil. For everyone who does evil hates the light, and doesn't come to the light (Jesus), lest his works would be exposed. But he who does the truth comes to the light (Jesus), that his works may be revealed, that they have been done in God."

May God bless you in the days ahead as you seek Jesus, His truth, and light.

I pray God will bless you whenever you read your Bible, pray, and fellowship with other believers. I pray you will find a church family you love, and you will seek to baptism, if you aren't baptized already.

Always remember, if you prayed the prayer asking Jesus to be your Lord, and you believe in Him, you are saved!

♥ CONGRATULATIONS! May God Bless YOU now and forever! ♥

*If you would like to help fellow seekers, please leave an honest review describing this study on Amazon.com. Just search for "Is Jesus God" on Amazon. Select this book in the search results, and post your review in the reviews section. Your honest description will help others decide if this study is one that will help them grow.

ABOUT THE AUTHOR

Sandra K. Cook (a.k.a. Sandy) became a Christian when a door-to-door evangelism came to tell her about Jesus. She was saved on the front doorstep of her home when she was in the 10th grade, and she asked Jesus to become Lord of her life.

Sandy's life changed throughout the years that followed by enduring fiery trials. Sandy married at 19, became a widow at 22, lived in poverty, was assaulted, and in a bank robbery with a gun held to her head. Sandy was suicidal, struggled with her self-esteem, and felt her life was pointless.

At the time of her first husband's death, Sandy began to read her Bible from cover-to-cover. She was deeply desiring to learn about God, the meaning of life, and her purpose. Reading the Bible set Sandy's heart on walking with the Lord. She was gripped by the love God proclaims for each of us, because she often felt unloved and unlovable.

In her life today, Sandy focuses on godly love, above all things. She seeks to help other Christians grow their fruit of the spirit. She believes everybody is more than somebody.. Everybody is God's Beloved Child.

The greatest joys in Sandy's life are spending time with her husband, sons, family, and her friends. Sandy loves reading to learn, studying the Bible, photography, and singing praise songs. Although, she loves singing, you do not want to hear her tone deaf renditions!

Sandy earned her Degree of Divinity from the Christian Leaders Institute. Sandy is a certified Biblical Life Coach. She also has a Master's Degree in Instructional Design, and is a life-long learner.

Sandy prays God will richly bless YOU in your life! ♥

OTHER BOOKS BY SANDY K. COOK

WHO IS JESUS?

IS JESUS THE SAVIOR?

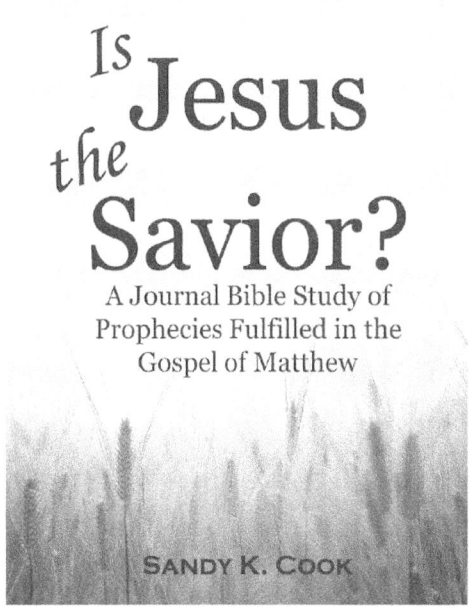

IS JESUS REAL?

BE A PERSON AFTER GOD'S OWN HEART

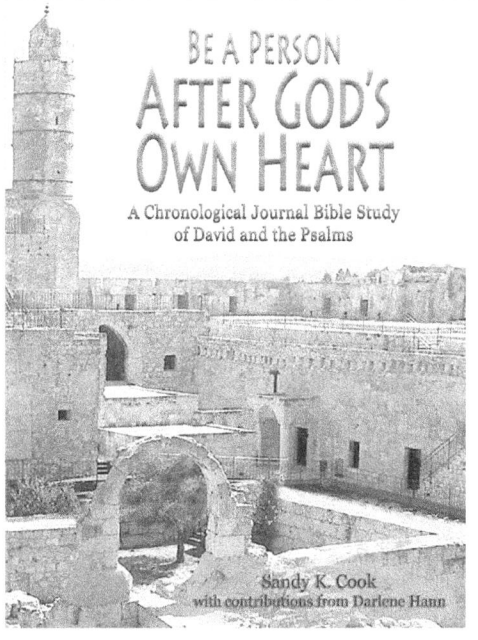

www.ingramcontent.com/pod-product-compliance
Lightning Source LLC
Chambersburg PA
CBHW081744100526
44592CB00015B/2291